WITHDRAWN

RANDOM HOUSE TREASURY ✍

FAVORITE POEMS
FROM CITIES AROUND THE WORLD

RANDOM HOUSE TREASURY

FAVORITE POEMS
FROM CITIES AROUND
THE WORLD

VICTORIA SAMS, EDITOR

RANDOM HOUSE
REFERENCE

NEW YORK

Random House Treasury of Favorite Poems from Cities Around the World
Copyright © 2004 by Victoria Sams

This book is available for special discounts for bulk purchases for sales promotions or premiums. Special editions, including personalized covers, excerpts of existing books, and corporate imprints, can be created in large quantities for special needs. For more information, write to Special Markets/Premium Sales, 1745 Broadway, MD 6-2, New York, NY, 10019 or e-mail specialmarkets@randomhouse.com.

Please address inquiries about electronic licensing of reference products, for use on a network or in software or on CD-ROM, to the Subsidiary Rights Department, Random House Reference, fax 212-572-6003.

Visit the Random House Web site: www.randomhouse.com

Typeset and printed in the United States of America.

Library of Congress cataloging-in-publication data is available.

ISBN 0-375-72074-x

First Edition
0 9 8 7 6 5 4 3 2 1

CONTENTS ❧

vi   INTRODUCTION

1   Cities in Dreams

9   Cities in Action

73   Cities in Trauma

113   Cities of Souls

145   Cities at Rest

183   Cities in the Past

221   Modern Cities

242   ABOUT THE POETS

274   PERMISSIONS ACKNOWLEDGMENTS

278   AUTHOR INDEX

279   CITY INDEX

INTRODUCTION ❧

How many of us imagine how our lives would be different if we had grown up in (or if we moved to) a different place? Cities have a special pull on the imagination, as places of escape, or drama, or non-stop energy, or opportunity. We often describe cities as we would people, with hearts and arteries and spirits and personalities: We speak of friendly cities and "in-your-face" cities, cities with a past, and cities without a soul. My aim in choosing the poems for this treasury was to find a group of poems that present as varied a picture of city life as possible. Attempting to do so has been a delicious and overwhelming task. A glance at anthologies devoted to New York or Singapore or Paris reveals the infinite possibilities contained within one city. Expand your poetic itinerary to a world tour and those options become staggering.

The poems in this book perform double duty as travelogue and imaginary archaeology, poetically excavating cities ancient and modern, grand and modest, hectic and sedate. In these pages, thirteenth-century T'ung-ch'uan might bump up against Georgian Dublin or twentieth-century Buenos Aires. Inspired by Italo Calvino's *Invisible Cities* and Salman Rushdie's *Imaginary Homelands*, I have structured this treasury around the ways that cities inhabit us—our imaginations and our memories—whether or not we happen to inhabit them. The categories are meant to embrace the ways in which cities shape our lives and our dreams.

Reading these poems may give you a fresh perspective on a familiar city, or inspire your attachment to an unknown cityscape. They may provoke laughter, nostalgia, anger, shock, or sympathy (perhaps all of these at once). I hope that you find them as compelling and rewarding as I do.

VICTORIA SAMS
Carlisle, Pennsylvania

CITIES IN DREAMS ❧

Block City

What are you able to build with your blocks?
Castles and palaces, temples and docks.
Rain may keep raining, and others go roam,
But I can be happy and building at home.

Let the sofa be mountains, the carpet be sea,
There I'll establish a city for me:
A kirk and a mill and a palace beside,
And a harbor as well where my vessels may ride.

Great is the palace with pillar and wall,
A sort of a tower on top of it all,
And steps coming down in an orderly way
To where my toy vessels lie safe in the bay.

This one is sailing and that one is moored:
Hark to the song of the sailors on board!
And see on the steps of my palace, the kings
Coming and going with presents and things!

—*Robert Louis Stevenson*

On Lynn Terrace

All day to watch the blue wave curl and break,
  All night to hear it plunging on the shore—
In this sea-dream such draughts of life I take
    I cannot ask for more.

Behind me lie the idle life and vain,
  The task unfinished, and the weary hours;
That long wave softly bears me back to Spain
    And the Alhambra's towers!

Once more I halt in Andalusian Pass,
  To list the mule-bells jingling on the height;
Below, against the dull esparto grass,
    The almonds glimmer white.

Huge gateways, wrinkled, with rich grays and
      browns,
  Invite my fancy, and I wander through
The gable-shadowed, zigzag streets of towns
    The world's first sailors knew.

Or, if I will, from out this thin sea-haze
   Low-lying cliffs of lovely Calais rise;
Or yonder, with the pomp of olden days,
      Venice salutes my eyes.

Or some gaunt castle lures me up its stair;
   I see, far off, the red tiled hamlets shine,
And catch, through slits of windows here and
      there,
      Blue glimpses of the Rhine.

Again I pass Norwegian fjord and fell,
   And through bleak wastes to where the
      sunset's fires
Light up the white-walled Russian citadel,
      The Kremlin's domes and spires.

And now I linger in green English lanes,
   By garden-plots of rose and heliotrope;
And now I face the sudden pelting rains
      On some lone Alpine slope.

Now at Tangier, among the packed bazaars,
    I saunter, and the merchants at the doors
Smile, and entice me: here are jewels like stars,
    And curved knives of the Moors;

Cloths of Damascus, strings of amber dates;
    What would Howadji—silver, gold, or stone?
Prone on the sun-scorched plain outside the gates
    The camels make their moan.

All this is mine, as I lie dreaming here,
    High on the windy terrace, day by day;
And mine the children's laughter, sweet and clear,
    Ringing across the bay.

For me the clouds; the ships sail by for me;
    For me the petulant sea-gull takes its flight;
And mine the tender moonrise on the sea,
    And hollow caves of night.

—*Thomas Bailey Aldrich*

ONE CITY ONLY

One city only, of all I have lived in,
And one house of that city, belong to me …
I remember the mellow light of afternoon
Slanting across brick buildings on the waterfront,
And small boats at rest on the floating tide,
And larger boats at rest in the near-by harbor;
And I know the tidal smell, and the smell of mud,
Uncovering oyster flats, and the brown bare
    toes of small negroes
With the mud oozing between them;
And the little figures leaping from log to log,
And the white children playing among them—
I remember how I played among them—
And I remember the recessed windows of the
    gloomy halls
In the darkness of decaying grandeur,
The feel of cool linen in the cavernous bed,
And the window curtain swaying gently

In the night air;
All the half-hushed noises of the street
In the southern town,
And the thrill of life—
Like a hand in the dark
With its felt, indeterminate meaning:
I remember that I knew there the stirring of
    passion,
Fear, and the knowledge of sin,
Tragedy, laughter, death....

And I remember too, on a dead Sunday afternoon
In the twilight,
When there was no one else in the house,
My self suddenly separated itself
And left me alone,
So that the world lay about me, lifeless.

I could not touch it, or feel it, or see it;
Yet I was there.
The sensation lingers:
Only the most vital threads
Hold me at all to living …
Yet I only live truly when I think of that house;
Only enter then into being.
One city only of all I have lived in,
And one house of that city, belong to me.

—*Alice Corbin*

CITIES IN ACTION ❧

On a Subway Express

I, who have lost the stars, the sod,

For chilling pave and cheerless light,
Have made my meeting-place with God

A new and nether Night—

Have found a fane where thunder fills

Loud caverns tremulous;—and these
Atone me for my reverend hills

And moonlit silences.

A figment in the crowded dark,

Where men sit muted by the roar,
I ride upon the whirring Spark

Beneath the city's floor.

In this dim firmament, the stars

Whirl by in blazing files and tiers;
Kin meteors graze our flying bars,

Amid the spinning spheres.

Speed! speed! until the quivering rails

Flash silver where the head-light gleams,
As when on lakes the Moon impales

The waves upon its beams.

Life throbs about me, yet I stand

Outgazing on majestic Power;
Death rides with me, on either hand,

In my communion hour.

You that 'neath country skies can pray,

Scoff not at me—the city clod;—
My only respite of the Day

Is this wild ride—with God.

—*Chester Firkins*

Contrasts

The windows of my poetry are wide open on
   the boulevards and in the shop windows
Shine
The precious stones of light
Listen to the violins of the limousines and the
   xylophones of the linotypes
The sketcher washes with the hand-towel of the sky
All is color spots
And the hats of the women passing by are comets
in the conflagration of the evening

Unity
There's no more unity
All the clocks now read midnight after being
   set back ten
   Minutes
There's no more time.
There's no more money.
In the Chamber
They are spoiling the marvelous elements of
   raw material

In the bistro
The blue-shirted workers are drinking red wine
Every Saturday a chicken for game

People are playing
They are betting
From time to time a bandit goes by in a car
Or a child plays with the Arc de Triomphe …
I advise Mr. Pig to lodge his protégés in the
    Eiffel Tower.

Today
Change of ownership
The Holy Ghost is being retailed in the tiniest
    boutiques
I read with delight the strips of calico
Of poppy
Only the pumice stones of the Sorbonne never
    bloom

The 'Samaritaine' sign ploughs through the Seine
And near Saint-Séverin
I hear
The stubborn clanging of the street cars

It's raining electric light-globes
Montrouge Gare de L'Est Métro Nord-Sud
   tourist boats world
All has become halos
Depth
On the Rue de Buci you hear *L'Intransigeant*
   and *Paris-Sports*
The airport of the sky is now, all in flames,
   a painting by Cimabue
When in the foreground
Men are
Long
Black
Sad
And smoke, factory chimneys

—*Blaise Cendrars on Paris, France*

Bamako Poem

for manthia diawara and kamona knepp

·

at Timbuctu
atop the oldest mosque in the world
an ostrich egg still marks & mocks the moon

·

Timbuctu is a desert of buildings
. when the rain falls. there is no more desert
or rather there are no more buildings

·

only desert

·

at Gao
the shak-shak nims along the River Niger
greet the dawn

·

at Djenne
the mosque of the moon
is the oldest spoken poem in the world

•

at Bamako
coming off the long stem white stone bridge, its arch a rose
reflecting in the ancient pool. this middlepassage

of the River Niger. mother of waters. fishes. crescent
of the mule. a kora's fluid butter on the dry
dusty biscuit platter of the continent

hulls of the baobab are huge small houses for the poor
. store palaces of firewood. charcoal. plank
-tons of restruction going on no-where no-where.

dirt

-eating balls of market vitamins. tins finish
of their fish. less contents wrapt
cloth. bolted in thunder. a few flags flaring free.

dark

caves of indigo. beggars of charity & time. old
cast-off soldiers ruined by the harmattan some blind
. salt miners raddled w/the xaala in their flesh & mind

. ten thousand petit-malinke malis. fulfulde. jalon. fula peul.
come over this stone bridge & high-
way every morning from as far away as Kouliko

by lorry. bicycle. on fiat faith & motor scooter flinting.
. but mostly tall thin unsmiling squint-
ing men from distant alligator villages. dark ridges

of residual forest far out on the Saheel horizon
they walk in out of the long hoarse cloth
of the encroaching desert

in bouba cotonu. in simple thobe. trail-
ing their long distance sandalled feet
click clock. ing into Banks of marble mountain
the Hôtels of Citadel et Hirondelles. the cobalt Airline Offices
. the l'Ambassade de France. and the grave mundane maus-
oleums of the Govvamant
dancing in their brittle glancing chandeliers of glass

dew.

-drops of Timbuctu receive them in high sealing moon
-less rooms. and reel them. reel them
in from red dust hanamanta already rising pan
-ther in the hot heat open oven of the wave of day

.

a girl.
a little shave
-head five year old mos
-quitto tiéwarra

w/ golden earrings blink
-ing. in short blue fading poplin dress. gath
-ered up. a butter
-fly. at her bambara shoulders

into two blue poppin puffs. cute
tucked-in waist and w/ her pan
-ties showing what may be
the latest gamine style along the edges of the desert

.

on strong young slender leggo legs she stops to stoop
into the gutter of her play
where the stone bridge arching's welcome ends
near where a group of cement-stain construction workers sit.
and picks up. in like tender triumph
to her turning-to-her brother. a little scarcely older
. the round pale plastic cover of an ice cream can

.

what can you . can you
call these plastic round containers

not 'tin'. it isn't tin
at all. nor tinnin.

no
not 'can'.
not

really 'can'
that cannot be. bleeds
the wrong meaning from the cast-off

'cup' 'tin can container'
is too ample & too vague
-ly multi. litteral to cap the cup which also isnt
& too far from gar. bage dumps at Timbuctu

.

but notice how she doesn't care
she knows x/actly what the white cast-off containers do
she
has high hopes for this one here
this dusty flat. bush early morning frizzbee day.
as if she gone out
shopping early for a bargain piece of bogólan & fini mud-
cloth made by the egerou Serra women. or for a
brand
new shining aluminium kettle that has found its peace

.

along the sidewalk now
the two

. sister & scarcely older brother

the two
so close together. step in step

tick

-ing togather like bi
-cycle clicks

- only a pair of loving sibs cd run as one
like this in this

hard life of little fatten flesh over their Mali ribs
know

-ing the same shamba mother's milk her passion hip &
grip of market cloth the same small smelly narrow
pallet

in the straw hut thatch
the same dog barks & millet rustles in the dark

the same long hazy silky view of distant mountains
Ogotemmêli Bandigara
nearing in yr heart

.

their four legs pedal off
her little shoulders pump
-ing young & hopeful w/her brother in the light

blue poplin dress. high
puffed-up at the shoulders
like she high-five. in fives so far so far from
Timbuctu. this Bamako & katatora morning on the Niger

.

w/her moon

—*Kamau Brathwaite on Bamako, Mali*

Sandybrook Bus Terminus

Late autumn rain falls, the day ends early.
The trees lining the street stand bare, complain
  of the cold.
The last bus is just arriving at the Sandybrook
  terminus.
The late evening sky is dark and deep. The
  wind comes gusting,
piercing to the very bones. Labor done, a few
  people
get off the last bus. The tip of a dry branch
  sways in the wind.
To it the world is climbing to the branch's tip.
  And slipping back.
The world complains it's too slippery.
What? If cold air is overturned, warm air results?
The yard in front of the station is desolate. One
  old drunk
disappears, waddling like a goose. 'A bird flew
  over the cuckoo's nest.'
What? A bird! Movies? Ridiculous,
crumbling to pieces even in the dim lamplight,

the glittering sands and sandbanks of times past:
is someone trying to tear his breast open with
bare hands?
Waterlight can never conceive
that this world has tears clearer than water.
There, the sandy brookside people who live
embracing sandbanks
as if eager to uncover the depths of their sand:
all that remains in the net of the ground,
caught in the water, is sand.
The night flows past like water. Sitting on the sand
I listen all night long to nodding Sandybrook,
to its wheezing sounds.
Standing at the far end of the bus terminus.

—*Ch'on Yang-Hui (translation by Suh Sook and
Brother Anthony) on Seoul, Korea*

*Note: Sandybrook and Waterlight are English place names
corresponding to Moraenae and Susaek, two neighbor-
hoods in western Seoul whose names the poet plays with in
this poem.*

Impression du Matin

The Thames nocturne of blue and gold

Changed to a harmony in grey;

A barge with ochre-coloured hay
Dropt from the wharf: and chill and cold

The yellow fog came creeping down

The bridges, till the houses' walls

Seemed changed to shadows, and St. Paul's
Loomed like a bubble o'er the town

Then suddenly arose the clang

Of waking life; the streets were stirred

With country wagons; and a bird
Flew to the glistening roofs and sang.

But one pale woman all alone,

The daylight kissing her wan hair,

Loitered beneath the gas lamps' flare
With lips of flame and heart of stone.

—*Oscar Wilde on London, England*

A Description of a City Shower

Careful observers may fortell the hour
(By sure prognostics) when to dread a shower:
While rain depends, the pensive cat gives o'er
Her frolics, and pursues her tail no more.
Returning home at Night, you'll find the sink
Strike your offended sense with double stink.
If you be wise, then go not far to dine,
You spend in coach hire more than save in wine.
A coming shower your shooting corns presage,
Old aches throb, your hollow tooth will rage.
Sauntering in coffeehouse is Dulman seen;
He damns the climate and complains of spleen.
   Meanwhile the south rising with dabbled wings,
A sable cloud a-thwart the welkin flings,
That swilled more liquor than it could contain,
And, like a drunkard, gives it up again.
Brisk Susan whips her linen from the rope,
While the first drizzling shower is born aslope,
Such is that sprinkling which some careless quean*

*wench

Flirts on you from her mop, but not so clean.
You fly, invoke the Gods; then turning, stop
To rail; she singing, still whirls on her mop.
Not yet, the dust had shunned the unequal strife,
But aided by the wind, fought still for life;
And wafted with its foe by violent gust,
'Twas doubtful which was rain, and which was
  dust.
Ah! where must needy poet seek for aid,
When dust and rain at once his coat invade?
Sole coat, where dust cemented by the rain,
Erects the Nap, and leaves a cloudy stain.

Now in contiguous drops the flood comes down,
Threatening with deluge this devoted town.
To shops in crowds the dagled* females fly,
Pretend to cheapen goods, but nothing buy.
The Templer* spruce, while every spout's abroach,

*mud-spattered, *law student

Stays till 'tis fair, yet seems to call a Coach.
The tucked-up sempstress walks with hasty
    strides,
While streams run down her oiled umbrella's
    sides.
Here various kinds by various fortunes led,
Commence acquaintance underneath a shed.
Triumphant Tories, and desponding Whigs,
Forget their feuds, and join to save their wigs.
Boxed in a chair the beau impatient sits,
While spouts run clattering o'er the roof by fits;
And ever and anon with frightful din
The leather sounds, he trembles from within.
So when Troy chairmen bore the wooden steed,
Pregnant with Greeks impatient to be freed,
(Those bully Greeks, who, as the moderns do,
Instead of paying chairmen, run them through,)
Laocoön struck the outside with his spear,
And each imprisoned hero quaked for fear.

Now from all parts the swelling kennels* flow,
And bear their trophies with them as they go:
Filth of all hues and odours seem to tell
What streets they sailed from, by their sight
    and smell.
They, as each torrent drives, with rapid force
From Smithfield, or St. Pulchre's shape their
    course,
And in huge confluence joined at Snow-Hill ridge,
Fall from the conduit prone to Holborn-Bridge.
Sweepings from butchers' stalls, dung, guts, and
    blood,
Drowned puppies, stinking sprats*, all
    drenched in mud,
Dead cats and turnip tops, come tumbling down
    the flood.

—*Jonathan Swift on London, England*

*gutters, *small fish

Glasgow Sonnets

I

A mean wind wanders through the backcourt
  trash.
Hackles on puddles rise, old mattresses
puff briefly and subside. Play-fortresses
of brick and bric-a-brac spill out some ash.
Four storeys have no windows left to smash,
but in the fifth a chipped sill buttresses
mother and daughter the last mistresses
of that black block condemned to stand,
  not crash.
Around them the cracks deepen, the rats crawl.
The kettle whimpers on a crazy hob.
Roses of mould grow from ceiling to wall.
The man lies late since he has lost his job,
smokes on one elbow, letting his coughs fall
thinly into an air too poor to rob.

II

A shilpit* dog fucks grimly by the close.
Late shadows lengthen slowly, slogans fade.
The YY PARTICK TOI* grins from its shade
like the last strains of some lost *libera nos
a malo*. No deliverer ever rose
from these stone tombs to get the hell they made
unmade. The same weans* never make the grade.
The same grey street sends back the ball it throws.
Under the darkness of a twisted pram
a cat's eyes glitter. Glittering stars press
between the silent chimney-cowls and cram
the higher spaces with their SOS.
Don't shine a torch on the ragwoman's dram.
Coats keep the evil cold out less and less.

*puny, *Partick-based gang, *children

III

'See a tenement due for demolition?
I can get ye rooms in it, two, okay?
Seven hundred and nothin legal to pay
For it's no legal, see? That's my proposition,
ye can take it or leave it but. The position
is simple, you want a hoose, I say
for eight hundred pounds it's yours.' And they,
trailing five bairns, accepted his omission
of the foul crumbling stairwell, windows wired
not glazed, the damp from the canal, the cooker
without pipes, packs of rats that never tired—
any more than the vandals bored with snooker
who stripped the neighbouring houses, howled,
    and fired
their aerosols—of squeaking 'Filthy lucre!'

IV

Down by the brickworks you get warm at least.
Surely soup-kitchens have gone out? It's not
the Thirties now. Hugh MacDiarmid forgot
in 'Glasgow 1960' that the feast
of reason and the flow of soul have ceased
to matter to the long unfinished plot
of heating frozen hands. We never got
an abstruse song that charmed the raging beast.
So you have nothing to lose but your chains,
dear Seventies. Dalmarnock, Maryhill,
Blackhill and Govan, better sticks and stanes
Should break your banes, for poets' words are ill
to hurt ye. On the wrecker's ball the rains
of greeting cities drop and drink their fill.

V

'Let them eat cake' made no bones about it.
But we say let them eat the hope deferred
and that will sicken them. We have preferred
silent slipways to the riveters' wit.
And don't deny it—that's the ugly bit.
Ministers' tears might well have launched a herd
of bucking tankers if they'd been transferred
from Whitehall to the Clyde. And smiles don't fit
either. 'There'll be no bevvying' said Reid
at the work-in. But all the dignity you muster
can only give you back a mouth to feed
and rent to pay if what you lose in bluster
is no more than win patience with 'I need'
while distant blackboards use you as their duster.

VI

The North Sea oil-strike tilts east Scotland up,
and the great sick Clyde shivers in its bed.
But elegists can't hang themselves on fled—
from trees or poison a recycled cup—
If only a less faint, shaky sunup
glimmered through the skeletal shop and shed
and men washed round the piers like gold and
   spread
golder in soul than Mitsubishi or Krupp—
The images are ageless but the thing
is now. Without my images the men
ration their cigarettes, their children cling
to broken toys, their women wonder when
the doors will bang on laughter and a wing
over the firth be simply joy again.

VII

Environmentalists, ecologists
and conservationists are fine no doubt.
Pedestrianization will come out
fighting, riverside walks march off the lists,
pigeons and starlings be somnambulists
in far-off suburbs, the sandblaster's grout
multiply pink piebald facades to pout
at sticky-fingered mock-Venetianists.
Prop up's the motto. Splint the dying age.
Never displease the watchers from the grave.
Great when fake architecture was the rage,
but greater still to see what you can save.
The gutted double fake meets the adage:
a wig's the thing to beat both beard and shave.

VIII

Meanwhile the flyovers breed loops of light
in curves that would have ravished tragic Toshy—
clean and unpompous, nothing wishy-washy.
Vistas swim out from the bulldozer's bite
by day, and banks of earthbound stars at night
begin. In Madame Emé's Sauchie Haugh, she
could never gain in leaves or larks or sploshy
lanes what's lost in a dead boarded site—
the life that overspill is overkill to.
Less is not more, and garden cities are
The flimsiest oxymoron to distil to.
And who wants to distil? Let bus and car
and hurrying umbrellas keep their skill to
Feed ukiyo-e beyond Lochnagar.

IX

It groans and shakes, contracts and grows again.
Its giant broken shoulders shrug off rain.
It digs its pits to a shauchling refrain.
Roadworks and graveyards like their gallus men.
It fattens fires and murders in a pen
and lets them out in flaps and squalls of pain.
It sometimes tears its smoky counterpane
to hoist a bleary fist at nothing, then
at everything, you never know. The west
could still be laid with no one's tears like dust
and barricaded windows be the best
to see from till the shops, the ships, the trust
return like thunder. Give the Clyde the rest.
Man and the sea make cities as they must.

X

From thirtieth floor windows at Red Road
he can see choughs and samphires, dreadful trade—
the schoolboy reading *Lear* has that scene made.
A multi is a sonnet stretched to ode
and some say that's no joke. The gentle load
of souls in clouds, vertiginously stayed
above the windy courts, is probed and weighed.
Each monolith stands patient, ah'd and oh'd.
And stalled lifts generating high-rise blues
can be set loose. But stalled lives never budge.
They linger in the single-ends that use
their spirit to the bone, and when they trudge
from closemouth to laundrette their steady shoes
carry a world that weighs us like a judge.

—*Edwin Morgan on Glasgow, Scotland*

Chicago

Hog Butcher for the World,
Tool Maker, Stacker of Wheat,
Player with Railroads and the Nation's
  Freight Handler;
Stormy, husky, brawling,
City of the Big Shoulders;

They tell me you are wicked and I believe them,
  for I
Have seen your painted women under the gas
  lamps
luring the farm boys.
And they tell me you are crooked and I answer:
  Yes, it
is true I have seen the gunman kill and go free to
kill again.
And they tell me you are brutal and my reply
  is: On the

Faces of women and children I have seen the marks
Of wanton hunger.
And having answered so I turn once more to
those who
sneer at this my city, and I give them back the
sneer
and say to them:
Come and show me another city with lifted
head singing
so proud to be alive and coarse and strong and
cunning.
Flinging magnetic curses amid the toil of piling
job on
job, here is a tall bold slugger set vivid against the
little soft cities;
Fierce as a dog with tongue lapping for action,
cunning
as a savage pitted against the wilderness.

Bareheaded,
Shoveling,
Wrecking,
Planning,
Building, breaking, rebuilding,
Under the smoke, dust all over his mouth,
   laughing with white teeth,
Under the terrible burden of destiny laughing
   as a young man laughs,
Laughing even as an ignorant fighter laughs
   who has never lost a battle,
Bragging and laughing that under his wrist is the
pulse, and under his ribs the heart of the people,
Laughing!
Laughing the stormy, husky, brawling laughter
   of Youth, half-naked, sweating, proud to be Hog
Butcher, Tool Maker, Stacker of Wheat,
   Player with
Railroads and Freight Handler to the Nation.

—*Carl Sandburg on Chicago, Illinois*

China is Floating Past Me

China is floating past me, and I watch not
The little isles, the cool jade-rippling bay.
Half yesterday her face. Yes, I shall reckon
Her laugh, her terror, things of yesterday,
Seeing them vaguely, from so far away,
Coldly from west's grey eyes and unawoken
Saying not for me is brilliant, or is broken
Lord butterfly on lord hibiscus spray—

And not for passing guests are set in motion
Junks that are autumn leaves across the ocean.

I shall be chaptered in the books of stone
The cities of the west, aloof, immense
With arrogance the marrow of their bone
And speed the levin* of their insolence;
There to walk undisguised, without pretence

*lightning

Of lowlier love than in their fortresses
Is coldly fed: where even music is
A metal mouth, writhing open in a hiss
For new attack, where there is no defence.

Steadily I shall seek to keep in tune
All I shall say, with all that blears their noon.

The Hong Kong water, lapping on stone stairs
Where a young lemming tipped the evening tide;
A broken moon, frail white, a lamp for prayers
So softly said, immaculate from pride
It mattered not if granted or denied
The fragile wish: and said to low for mortals,
The waters' quiet petition at the portal
Of the black cave that cracked across the west
To bear a pearly sampan on its breast.

—*Robin Hyde on Hong Kong*

London

Athwart the sky a lowly sigh
    From west to east the sweet wind carried;
The sun stood still on Primrose Hill;
    His light in all the city tarried;
The clouds on viewless columns bloomed
Like smouldering lilies unconsumed.

"Oh sweetheart, see! How shadowy,
Of some occult magician's rearing,
Or swung in space of heaven's grace
    Dissolving, dimly reappearing,
Afloat upon ethereal tides
St. Paul's above the city rides!"

A rumor broke through the thin smoke,
    Enwreathing abbey, tower, and palace,
The parks, the squares, the thoroughfares,
    The million-peopled lanes and alleys,
An ever-muttering prisoned storm,
The heart of London beating warm.

—*John Davidson on London, England*

Samarkand, and Other Markets I Have Known

For Naguib Mafouz

"The world is a market place…" —*Yoruba song*

"We take the Golden Road to Samarkand"
—*James Elroy Flecker*, Hassan

I
A market is kind haven for the wandering soul
Or the merely ruminant. Each stall
Is shrine and temple, magic cave of memorabilia.
Its passages are grottoes that transport us,
Bargain hunters all, from pole to antipodes,
   annulling
Time, evoking places and lost histories.
A market is where Samarkand invades
Johannesburg, and, as the shutters close,
Departs without regrets or trace

Until its next reincarnation. A market is
Where London's Portobello spells
Caracas and Yoruba, Catalan or Khourassan,
And though hard currency is what changes hands,
It lets you drift in fluid channels where
Sensations thrive on trade by barter.

Chimes of faith assail the market place—
The muezzin's prayer alert, a shrine within
    the warren,
A lean-to church dispenses chants at war
With handbells. White-robed dervishes in trance
At crossroads of Spices Row and Fabric Lane
Swirl, oblivious to slender saffron files
Meandering, equally oblivious to the world.
Fairy-bells in counterpoint to cosmic *ooms*—
Hare Krishna's other dervishes in slight

Ethereal motion through the firewood stalls.
Deep in the maze of Isale-eko*, Buddhist mantras?

The *orisa** faithful wait their turn. In season,
Ogun's iron bells, Sango's *ayan* drums
Oya's chalk and coral maids reclaim
This borrowed space. Ancestral voice ascendant,
Masks of wood and webbed visors, indigo and
   camwood
Presences unfold their mats of invocation.

These are the markets I have known,
Tibetan souls on pilgrimage to shrines
In heartlands of Dogon, Baule or Zululand.
Leaflets of salvation for the unwary
Barefoot evangelists of every faith
Tuned to bared moments of the vacant soul.

*Lagos suburb, *guardian spirits

Let all contend. Let a hundred thousand
Flowers diffuse exotic incense and a million
Stars perfume the sky, till the infant cry of Truth
Resound in the market of the heart,
And warring faiths
Reconcile in one immensity of Being.

Trade and holy places, saints and salesmen
Have ever lived as soul companions, caterers
For the needs of flesh and spirit—bread
And wafer, wine and holy water, homilies,
Talismans and rosaries, the blessed
Pouch of earth or magic mantras, locks
And lockets of painted mystics
Reliquaries and tourist souvenirs around
A healing spring, a spot of revelation—
The pilgrim trade is evenly sanctified.
Still, here and there, one lashes out—recall
The prince of peace turned manic in a synagogue

Turned market place? Lashed trespassers
With tongue and whip? That lash, in retrospect,
Was kind. I envy the usurers of old
The wages of their sin and mine. Our seasons'
Lesser desecrations—a face unveiled,
An ankle bared, a keepsake, taste or thought
Of *foreign* taint—feed Grim Reaper Purity
From lethal thrusts, not the symbolic lash.
They pierce the heart, not touch the soul within.

Go to the orisa and be wise. Ifa
Shuns the excluding tongue, unveils
Uncharted routes to knowledge, truth
And godhead. Man is restless seeker,
What follows six, says Ifa, transcends the bounds
Of seven—there are no final rites to numerology.
Let who can, count the motes in a sunbeam
Or weigh the span of grief from voice to voice

In the home of the immolated.
Go to the orisa. None but fools
Claim guardianship of the final gateway.

II

Now—take a hidden turn between the stalls—
A curtain parts. The wares within are never on display
Ranged out of sight, awaiting clientele that know
The secret maps of every market place.
Fumes that ransack, then bare the mind
To ecstasies unknown in ancient Samarkand—
These seekers also ply uncharted routes
To the outer markets of the world, dissolve
In sunspots trapped in pin-points of their eyes,
Regaining wholeness only they know where.
Tubes and needles reign supreme. The crucible
Is sacrament and host to cravings

When the makeshift stove is lit.
Or enter where the sheen on beaten brass gives way
To a glint on the Gatling gun, still serviceable.
Or a shoulder-held dispatcher, lethal cone
On end, and oil wraps masking ingenuities
That pave the shortest way to hell. Still,
Hell's location is a space of choice. In open air,
Dante weds Fayed on ancient trestles
Browned with age, pages still uncut as if
To hide profanities of afterlife as dreamt
By poets and lunatics, moralists and lovers.
A slumbering virgin, timeless, but her youth
   preserved
And you the wandering prince to whom
Her thighs slit open for a gentle ravishing.

And Samarkand? O Samarkand!
I cannot stroll through markets but I dread

Lest I see Samarkand again, yet long to see
How exchange has merged with change, see
If the ageless geese on tattered slippers
In Utopia—the *lumpen prol.*, midwives
Of new breed of being, named the world's
Inheritors—have at last metamorphosed
Into princesses and masters of the promised land.

Such feeble scarecrows to my market mammas
Of Accra, Abidjan, Huambo, Cairo, Ibadan,
Plump mistresses of markets' riotous fare. Queens
Of fiesta, theatrics, courts of arbitration, crèche,
    but—
Wait! I summon witnesses to counter cries of bias:
Randy Weston, Oscar Peterson, hear them celebrate
Nigerian Marketplace, keyboards wild and wind
    on fire!
And strangers' brushes, daubing oils for dyes

In vain to trap the market's rainbow spectrum, bear
The weight of human tumult and the smell of life.
(It's there I pictured him, Mafouz, his soul in tune
With priests and pedlars of the *souk*.)

So much for ancient times—today the strings are muted.
Samarkand's sibling markets on these continents
Have fallen to dry dirges, dropped
To thin laments beneath collapsing thatch.
To make a killing on the market now
May prove too literal, where zealots strut as middlemen
To market lords of unseen paradise.

III
O Samarkand. Remember Samarkand? It was

That time of Utopia by the text. Eagerly
We crowded on the promise of a legend, found
A straw masquerade, the terminus of Party lies,
Inhuman patience that began in Moscow's streets
And wound through regulations and officialdom
To stagnate in Flecker's land of dreams.
There were no chants extolling market wares.
The bloom we sought in peasant cheeks.
Was lodged in hoards of produce crushed against
Deep warehouse vaults—tubers, pears, deep purple
Aubergines, ponderous cabbages and lean spices.
Destination—Party ranks and dachas by the sea.
The shine we sought upon their skin was locked
In racked tomatoes, straight from still-life
    canvases,
In melon sphericals, like new-discovered worlds.
A wild assault of rare, exotic fruits flared

Our questing nostrils, mocked the mien of stiff
Official guides, breezes from a different time
   and place—
We did ask questions; received responses by the
   text.
Joy had fled the faces of the eternal women.
They lined the market outskirts, silently,
Winter twigs, dark shadows framed in rags
Limp greens outstretched, limp socks and shawls—
The regulation surplus they could hawk at will
For those few kopeks they would call their own.
A market! And no human sounds? We bade adieu
To Samarkand; we shared the train that hauled
Her missing cries to Moscow's hidden stores.

From frying-pan to furnace, from Slough of
   Despond
To turbid ponds named law of market forces

That makes the outlaw Bullfrog of the bog—
   I dread
A Mafia kingdom where Samarkand is but
Another tame protectorate, yet on parade
As a consumer's paradise, where one will yearn
For those bedraggled hands of dead Utopia.
Their merchandise was theirs—to make and sell
Their leisure moments knit the shawl and spun
   the lace
Carved the likeness of grotesque of dreams.
Each offering was a flight from drudgery,
   a cunning hour
Defiant of lies, of regulations that imposed
   conformity.
At worst, a pittance earned, an elixir of escape.

I spurn this double counterfeit—wages earned
In goods from plant assemblage—brassieres,

Jars of mayonnaise, jockstraps, plated cutlery,
    diapers,
Negligées and curtain rods, shaving cream,
    deodorants
Tourist wares, the ever-replicating *babushka*…
Where barter is debased, and leisure must be shared
In after hours converting wages-merchandise
To a common currency devalued from the source.
O Samarkand, your workers must prove traders
    too?
Accosting strangers, plying second-tier exchange
Lest the home be starved! Samarkand,
What bargain you have made! Utopia sold for this?
Will Chernobyl pay wageless scientists
In enriched uranium, to solve the state's insolvency?

Or maybe—as Allah wills—since soul and sale
Have ever shared their space—Samarkand
Will turn the other sort, twin face of that

Tarnished paradise whose sauce for goose
Was not for gander. We bid adieu to
Kulak, comprador, bourgeois deviationist
Revisionist capitalist running dog false consciousness
And allied Gulag overtures that masked
The silent guest in every home. That doomsday
Noise is stilled. New heroes of the revolution
Hail the anointed text, now simplified, that reads:
Holy or unclean. Taboos proliferate.
Like the bazaars of Beirut, Algiers
Or Teheran, will a store display, an order form,
'Satanic' music, poster, a fable on a tapestry,
A catalogue of books, second-hand merchandise
A dog-eared copy of *Arabian Nights*, a pamphlet
    poem—
Prove the trader's violent passport into paradise?

IV
The bazaars of the *souk* may prove denuded

The magic carpet folded out of sight, in dread.

There may be new commissars on patrol

Messengers between the laity and Deity.

The scrambled word that passes censorship is—

Kill. Kill the unveiled, for the word is veiled

To all but the anointed few, dacoits of Deity.

They sanctify the blade, still dripping from its
   last jihad

It carves a path through an old man's neck, but

The moving finger writes ... though the ink of
   Kandahar

Has turned to blood. The heir of ancient dynasties

Of letters ... Khorassan, Alexandria, Timbuktoo ...
   lies sprawled

In the dirt and dust of a passageway.

He is no alien. No roots than his grow deeper

In that market place, no eye roved closer home.

He is that fixture in the market-place café

Sipping sweetened cups of mint, oblivious to
The bitter one that would be served
By the shadowy one, the waiter-stalker, a youth
Fed on dreams of sarabands of houris,
Doe-eyed virgins, wine and sweetmeats in the
    afterlife—
But to this paradise a key—the plunging knife.
    It's time to raise the rafters, time
    To chant the primal sanctity of man
    Beyond coarse politics, beyond meagerness
    Of race and faith, time to disinherit
    Nationhood, episcopacies—we declare
    This questing biped heir to cosmic legacies.
    Who kills for love of god kills love, kills god.
    Who kills in name of god leaves god,
    Without a name.

The market place of hate is quartered on the
    pious tongue

But this the old man knew, yet kept his daily tryst
With haggling cries, mock wars of merchandise
Mint tea and gossip, an avocation to observe
   and chronicle.
He shares the dreams of Samarkand
With traders and the traded, with sinners
And the sinned against,
With infidels and the self-assured of paradise—
A dream that never ends, a glimpse that still recedes,
That shimmering Golden Road to Samarkand.

V

The ocean meets the sea in a market place
And rivers ground their debris on its shelves—
Rich silt, beachcombers' treasure trove.
The rainbow's arc is rounded in a market place
Where scattered tribes of a busy world unite
Amidst the silenced blades of swords and spears
And ancient muskets, poison shafts and knobkerries.

Like guardians to that lost, miraculous edition,
Filled with lost wisdoms, lost journeys of the mind.
The space of dreams remain inviolate
Egalitarian in the market place
Though desecration stalks in priestly garb
By surrogates, by one-eyed arbiters.
But now we share the strange and marvelous,
Indulge in thoughts of origin. We people artefacts
From ivory, skin and herbs, from aromatic wood,
Sifts of powder guaranteed for ailments old
  and new
Dark mysteries in clay jars, beauty gels,
Love potions, the lost gems of the world
And many more with fake luster, fake patina—
Like fake piety, they exact veneration—still,
In the market place, their patina is peace, and
Though innocence be sometimes lost or
  counterfeited,
We share the gods of distant lands, of ancient times

And the Market Muse by whose decree
The knives are sheathed, and guns
Are mostly spiked, or fallen silent.
You who have heard the ocean waves,
Or the cries of dead mariners from bleached
Muteness of shell and conch, learn also
Other sounds beneath the market wares
And haggling voices—siren songs from coral beads,
A child's initiation wail in barks of camwood,
   a priest's
Liturgy in rosaries of sandalwood, a chieftain's
Ululation in horsetail whisks and beaded canes.

Dirges of bereavement seep through ancient mats,
The ochre-smeared antique, or a faded photograph—
The frame of tarnished silver will be home
Soon to a stranger's face, in an alien household.
And thus, we jostle strangers who turn guests

and kin—
The market is that kind of meeting place.
The world is a market place—thus goes the song.
At close of market, in a sombre light,
Our feet will lead the way
Homewards, when eyes have closed for ever
On the next market day, and the indigo throng
Of all *orisa* wait to lead
Each seeker by the hand, into that last sanctuary
Across the arch of shadows.

One market day, in the *souk* of Cairo,
The zealot's counterfeiting hand did not triumph.
The moving finger writes, and having writ ... the mind
Survives to sing the way on the Golden Road
Where dreams of Samarkand outlive
Tomorrow's market day.

—*Wole Soyinka on Samarkand, Uzbekistan (and elsewhere)*

Lagos

Lagos you are dirty
Your sand is soiled
Your fruits pithy.

I am tied to you
in a strange land
by lines that queue up
for foodstuffs you
should be eating but
ship off to me here
where I stand on check
out lines and marvel
at the cost of one
paw paw, just one mango
singular, along and apart
from you my dirty city.
O Lagos, your streets
are packed and pollute

the air while here in
a smug smogged city
I choke.

Your cord cuts my throat.
I am hurt and I cry like
my Mami market mothers
who go home night after
night with the same tin pots.
Their food is rotting and
ought to be thrown out to
the birds and beasts of
the forest/but the lines!
O God, these lines are so long
and between the houses and
the foodstuffs so many palms
must be oiled.

Nairas are dripping with black gold
and yet a beggar man's lot is the
same/ He covers his shame as best
he can and little boys skip school.
A policeman holds his right hand out
a green car passes him dash. And we go
dash you dis and we go dash you dat
and mek we do business.

O Lagos, Lagos, ah say, you don tyah
fo dis? Yousef wey you de com fom?
Me, I lng for the cleanliness of
sand roads that breathe long in carefully
spaced intervals between cars running
wild like mustangs roaming the plains.
There are no drivers to speak of.
They have vanished over hills and
into gulleys.

The seeds have been planted. It is a
bitter harvest we reap. The deeds have
been done. What has been sown is the
flower of our calabashes on the eve of
harvest. If only the waters in the Marina
   If only the waves would whisper louder
   the secrets of her beaches I would know
all/

My harbour is named after a queen whose
son's footprints are planted like a bad
seed on the headdress of my children.
Lagos, lay your plans carefully. There
is no way to stop the rise of bicycles
and lorries, hopeful bodies and empty
pots. You divert dash for food, care
for business. We are not an oasis in a
dying desert/ Have we not learnt, o

Lagos, the sound of seductive songs
And sights that blind us
Between need and life there *must* be hope/

—*Rashidah Ismaili*

CITIES IN TRAUMA ❧

Go to Ahmedabad

Go walk the streets of Baroda,
go to Ahmedabad,
go breathe the dust
until you choke and get sick
with a fever no doctor's heard of.
Don't ask me
for I will tell you nothing
about hunger and suffering.

As a girl I learned
never to turn anyone away
from our door. Ma told me
give fresh water, good food,
nothing you wouldn't eat.
Hunger is when your mother
tells you years later
in America the doctor says
she is malnourished,

her bones are weak
because there was never enough
food for the children,
hers and the women who came
to our door with theirs.
The children must always be fed.
Hunger is when your mother is sick
in America because she wanted you
to eat well. Hunger is
when you walk down the streets of Ahmedabad
and instead of handing out
coins to everyone
you give them tomatoes, cucumbers,
and go home with your mouth
tasting of burnt eucalyptus leaves
because you've lost
your appetite.
And yet, I say nothing
about hunger, nothing.

I have friends everywhere.
This time we met after ten years.
Someone died.
Someone got married.
Someone just had a baby.
And I hold the baby
because he's crying,
because there's a strange rash
all over his chest
And my friend says
do you have a child? Why not?
When will you get married?
And the bus arrives
crowded with people hanging
out the doors and windows.
And her baby cries
in my arms, cries
so an old man wakes up and yells

at me: How could I let
my child get so sick?
Luckily, just then
someone tells a good joke.

I have friends everywhere.
This time we met after ten years.
And suffering is
when I walk around Ahmedabad
for this is the place
I always loved
this is the place
I always hated
for this is the place
I can never be at home in
this is the place
I will always be at home in.

Suffering is
when I'm in Ahmedabad
after ten years
and I learn for the first time
I will never choose
to live here. Suffering is
living in America
and not being able
to write a damn thing
about it. Suffering is
not for me to tell you about.

Go walk the streets of Baroda,
go to Ahmedabad
and step around the cow-dung
but don't forget
to look at the sky.
It's special in January,

You'll never see kites like these again
Go meet the people if you can
And if you want to know
about hunger, about suffering,
go live it for yourself.
When there's an epidemic,
when the doctor says
your brother may die soon,
your father may die soon—
don't ask me how it feels.
It does not feel good.
That's why we make
tea with tulsi leaves,
that's why there's always someone
who knows a good story.

—*Sujata Bhatt on Ahmedabad, India*

Damascus Diary

You come to Damascus
and later are reborn there
growing twice your size in minutes
Poetry tosses stars into your hands
Roses root in you
and you envy the love that children know
When sudden war erupts
you are ashamed not to be one of its heroes
War explodes in the mountains and sky
while you sit writing poetry
In Damascus?
By what right?
You were born and you grow
like love, roses, children and beauty
    in Damascus
By what right?
Clouds build in my mind
till the answer rains down

Like them I am born and I grow
with, before, and after them
for I'm not here as a tourist
I am Palestine
and through my love ... I am also Damascus

Beloved, I am ashamed to love
in the warring moments of Damascus
for the most beautiful men have gone
to the trenches of the north
My trenches are the newspapers
My guns—the articles I write
I am ashamed to love in the absence
of the most perfect men
Nor can I enter cafes
where each chair protests to me:
Here sat a fighter
who now lives in the mountains!
Beloved, if you see my father, ask him

why he taught me the art of poetry
instead of how to fight—
by what right?
Men, women, beautiful boys and lovely girls
all conspire to cleanse my blood
I am the Arab exhausted by humiliation
asking that my blood be purified
with luminous light and simplest love,
purest kisses
So what do I give in return
but these poems, Damascus?
If my blood pours with torrential love
how can I share it
except in print?

—*Rashid Husain on Damascus, Syria*
[translation by May Jayyusi and Naomi Shihab Nye]

LONDON

I wander thro' each charter'd street,
Near where the charter'd Thames does flow.
A mark in every face I meet
Marks of weakness, marks of woe.

In every cry of every man,
In every infant's cry of fear,
In every voice, in every ban,
The mind-forg'd manacles I hear.

How the chimney-sweeper's cry
Every blackening church appalls,
And the hapless soldier's sigh
Runs in blood down palace walls.

But most thro' midnight streets I hear
How the youthful harlot's curse
Blasts the new-born infant's tear,
And blights with plagues the marriage hearse.

—*William Blake on London, England*

Ford O' Kabul River

Kabul town's by Kabul river—
  Blow the bugle, draw the sword—
There I lef' my mate for ever,
  Wet an' drippin' by the ford.
  Ford, ford, ford o' Kabul river,
  Ford o' Kabul river in the dark!
  There's the river up and brimmin', an' there's
    'arf a squadron swimmin'
  'Cross the ford o' Kabul river in the dark.

Kabul town's a blasted place—
  Blow the bugle, draw the sword—
'Strewth I sha'n't forget 'is face
  Wet an' drippin' by the ford!
  Ford, ford, ford o' Kabul river,
  Ford o' Kabul river in the dark!
  Keep the crossing-stakes beside you, an' they
    will surely guide you
  'Cross the ford o' Kabul river in the dark.

Kabul town is sun and dust—
    Blow the bugle, draw the sword—
I'd ha' sooner drownded fust
    'Stead of 'im beside the ford.
    Ford, ford, ford o' Kabul river,
    Ford o' Kabul river in the dark!
    You can 'ear the 'orses threshin', you can 'ear
        the men a-splashin',
    'Cross the ford o' Kabul river in the dark.

Kabul town was ours to take—
    Blow the bugle, draw the sword—
I'd ha' left it for 'is sake—
    'Im that left me by the ford.
    Ford, ford, ford o' Kabul river,
    Ford o' Kabul river in the dark!
    It's none so bloomin' dry there; ain't you
        never comin' nigh there,
    'Cross the ford o' Kabul river in the dark?

Kabul town'll go to hell—
    Blow the bugle, draw the sword—
'Fore I see him 'live an' well—
    'Im the best beside the ford.
    Ford, ford, ford o' Kabul river,
    Ford o' Kabul river in the dark!
    Gawd 'elp 'em if they blunder, for their
        boots'll pull 'em under,
    By the ford o' Kabul river in the dark.

Turn your 'orse from Kabul town—
    Blow the bugle, draw the sword—
'Im an' 'arf my troop is down,
    Down an' drownded by the ford.
    Ford, ford, ford o' Kabul river,
    Ford o' Kabul river in the dark!
    There's the river low an' fallin', but it ain't no
        use o' callin'
    'Cross the ford o' Kabul river in the dark.

—*Rudyard Kipling on Kabul, Afghanistan*

Regarding the Appearance
of Sir Laurence Olivier as
Richard III in a Lahore Cinema

Across the hot scootered streets, past
The building mosque ('site for the first air-
conditioned mosque in Asia' says the board).
Through the betel-ruined walls
Up the stairs, beneath the ample-
bosomed, wide-hipped bending beauties, staring
From the posters, eyes wide with collyrium,
Around the green stucco goddess, a hound
Nuzzling her improbable breasts, we came
To the Grand Stalls, 'conditioned climate by Trane'.

Dodging the hard hail of our running world
We come to see that monstrous, glossy head
Stare watchful, devious from a different screen,
And we have heard the high imperious voice
Beat faintly, without meaning, in our ears:
But these coloured distractions find a home

Here, where the edges of those splendid words
Fall soft, like feathers, on unknowing ears,
But rage and treachery speak loud and clear
When this black scorpion crimps across our eyes.
For the language vaults our senses
But these painted figures bring
Time and reason's sure defences,
We understand this real king
Stalking the tinsel alleys of the screen
In garish anger.

—*Shahid Hosain on Lahore, Pakistan*

The Desert

The Diary of Beirut under Siege, 1982

I

1

The cities break up
The land is a train of dust
Only poetry knows how to marry this space.

2

No road to his house—the siege.
And the streets are graveyards;
   Far away a stunned moon
   Hangs on threads of dust
   Over his house.

3

I said: This street leads to our house. He said: No.
   You won't pass. And pointed his bullets at me.

Fine, in every street
   I have homes and friends.

4

Roads of blood,
  The blood a boy was talking about
  And whispering to his friends:
  Only some holes known as stars
  Remain in the sky.

5

The voice of the city is soft
The face of the city glows
Like a little boy telling his dreams to the night
And offering his chair to the morning.

6

They found people in sacks:
  One without a head
  One without a tongue or hands
  One strangled
  The rest without shape or names.
Have you gone mad? Please,
  Don't write about these things.

7

In a page of a book
Bombs see themselves,
Prophetic sayings and ancient wisdom see
    themselves,
Niches see themselves.
The thread of carpet words
Go through memory's needle
Over the city's face.

8

The killer
In the air
Swims in the city's wound—
    The wound is the fall
    That shakes with its name,
    With its bleeding name
Everything around us.
The houses leave their walls
And I am not I

9

There may come a time when you'll be
Accepted to live deaf and dumb, and perhaps
They'll let you mumble: death,
    Life, resurrection—
    And peace be upon you.

10

From the palm wine to the calmness of the
    desert … etc.
From the morning that smuggles its stomach
    and sleeps on the corpses of the refugees…etc.
From the streets, army vehicles, concentration
    of troops … etc.
From the shadows, men, women … etc.
From the bombs stuffed with the prayers of
    Muslims and infidels… etc.
From the flesh of iron that bleeds and sweats
    pus … etc.
From the fields that long for the wheat, the
    green and the workers … etc.

From the castles walling our bodies and
    bombarding us with darkness ... etc.
From the myths of the dead which speak of life,
    express life ... etc.
From the dark dark dark
I breathe, feel my body, search for you and him,
    myself and others,
And hang my death
Between my face and these bleeding words ... etc.

11
You will see
    Say his name
    Say I painted his face
    Stretch your hands to him
    Or smile
    Or say I was once sad
    Or say I was once happy
You will see
    There is no homeland ...

12

The killing has changed the city's shape—
  This rock
    Is a boy's head
    This smoke people breathing.

13

Everything sings of his exile/a sea
  Of blood—what
Do you expect from these mornings other than
  their veins sailing
In the mists, on the waves of the massacre?

14

Keep her company at night, stay longer with
  her at night,
She's placed death on her lap,
And turned over her days
  Like old papers.
Keep the last pictures
  Of her landscape.

She's turning in her own sand,
In a pool of sparks,
And on her body
She has scars of people crying.

15

Seeds are scattered in our land,
So keep the secret of this blood,
Fields that nourish our myths—
    I'm talking about the zest of the seasons
    About the lightning in space.

16

Bourje Square*—(inscriptions whispering their
    secrets
        to broken bridges ...)
Bourje Square—(memory looking for itself
        in fire and dust ...)

*city center

Bourje Square——(an open desert
    swept and dragged by the winds ...)
Bourje Square——(witchcraft
    to see corpses moving/their limbs
    in a backstreet/their ghosts
    in a backstreet/you hear them sighing ...)
Bourje Square——(west and east
    gallows standing,
    martyrs and guardians ...)
Bourje Square——(a trail
    of caravans: myrrh
        frankincense and musk
            and spices opening the festival ...)
Bourje Square——(a trail
    of caravans: thunder
        and explosion and lightning and
            hurricanes opening the festival...)

Bourje Square—(I have called this era
  by the name of this place)

17
— Corpses or rubble,
Beirut's face?
— Bells ringing or people screaming?
— A friend?
— You? Hello.
Have you been away? Just back? What's new?
— They killed a neighbour ... /
— ....

playing games/
— Your dice is stronger today,
— Luck/
      ....
    Dark
    And words dragging words

II

1

My era tells me bluntly:
You do not belong.
I answer bluntly:
I do not belong,
I try to understand you.
Now I am a shadow
Lost in the desert
And shelter in the tent of a skull.

2

The distance shrinks, a window recedes.
Daylight is a thread.
Snipped by my lungs to stitch the evening.

3

All I said about my life and death
Recurs in the silence
Of the stone under my head …

4

Am I full of contradictions? That is correct.
   Now I am a plant. Yesterday, when I was
      between fire and water,
   I was a harvest.
   Now I am a rose and live coal,
   Now I am the sun and the shadow
   I am not a god.
Am I full of contradictions? That is correct.

5

The door of my house is closed.
Darkness is a blanket:
   A pale moon comes with
   A handful of light
   My words fail
   To convey my gratitude.

6

He shuts the door
Not to trap his joy
… But to free his grief.

7

Whatever comes will be old
So take with you anything other than this
madness—get ready
    To stay a stranger.

8

The sun no longer rises
It covers its feet with straw
And slips away …

9

I expect death to come at night
    To cushion his lap with
        A rose

Tired of the dust covering the forehead of dawn
Tired of the breathing of people.

10
—The night descends (these are the papers he gave
    to the ink—morning's ink that never came)
The night descends on the bed (the bed of the
    lover who never came)
The night descends /not a sound (clouds. Smoke)
The night descends (someone has in his hands
    rabbits? Ants?)
The night descends (the wall of the building
    shakes. All the curtains are transparent)
The night descends, listens (the stars as the
    night knows are dumb, and the last trees at the
    end of the wall remember nothing of what the air
    said to their branches)
The night descends (the wind whispers to the
    windows)

The night descends (the light penetrates.
  A neighbour lies in his nakedness)
The night descends (two people. A dress holding
  a dress—and the windows are transparent)
The night descends (this is a whim: the moon
  complains to its trousers about what the
  lovers have always complained of)
The night descends (he relaxes in a pitcher
  filled with wine. No friends just one man
  turning in his glass)
The night descends (carries a few spiders, feels
  at ease with insects which are a pest only to
  houses/signs of light: an angel coming,
  missiles or invitations? Our women neighbours
  have gone on pilgrimage/come back less slim
  and more coquettish)
The night descends (he enters between the
  breasts of the days/our Women neighbours
  are my days)
The night descends (that sofa/that pillow: this is

an alleyway, this is a place)

The night descends (what shall we prepare?
   Wine? Meat, soup and bread? The night
   hides from us its appetite)

The night descends (he plays for a short while
   with his snails, with strange doves which
   came from an unknown land, and with the
   insects not mentioned in the chapters of the
   book about reproduction among different
   animal species)

The night descends (thunder—or is it the noise
   of angels coming on their horses?)

The night descends (he mumbles, turning in his
   glass ...)

11

Who would show me a planet
   To give me ink to write about my night?

12

He wrote a poem

(how can I convince him my future is a desert?)

He wrote a poem

(who will shake the stoneness of words off me?)

He wrote a poem

(you don't belong if you don't kill a brother)

He wrote a poem

(how can we understand this fugitive

language caught between the question

and the poem?)

He wrote a poem

(can the refugee dawn embrace its sun?)

He wrote a poem

(there's confusion between the sun's face

and the sky)

He wrote a poem (… /let him die …)

13

Should I talk? On what?
   In what direction?
I ask you, seagull flying in the blueness of the
   sea ...
   Who said I asked, who said
I'm gazing at the sea or talking to the seagull?

   I never was
   I never walked
   I never said ...

14

I'll contradict myself.
I'll add to my dictionary:
   I don't belong to my language, my mouth
   Not once was it my mouth.
Ah, star of destruction, blood rose.

15

I should have been torn to pieces, thrown in a
    forest fire
To light the road.
Friend,
Tiredness,
Give me your kind hand
Give me what your nights took from my bleeding sun.

16

Anything rejected by other eyes will be looked
    after by my eyes.
This is my friendship's promise to destruction.

17

Since I surrendered myself to myself and asked
    What is the difference between destruction
        and myself,
I have lived the poet's optimum life:
    No answer.

18

After poetry had torn time's dress
I called on the winds
To stitch the rags to the place.

19

What is it that touched Mutanabbi*
    Other than this soil that felt his tread?
He betrayed many things,
But not his vision.

20

You do not die because you are created
    Or because you have a body
You die because you are the face of the future.

21

Let
My dream neglect my body
And my body betray its floating sleeplessness

*Abbasid poet

22

I should call a wolf to shine the mirror of the sheep
 That forgot their own image.

23

We no longer meet,
Rejection and exile keep us apart.
The promises are dead, space is dead,
Death alone
Has become our meeting point.

24

The flower
 That tempted the wind to carry its perfume
Died yesterday.

25

My tiredness sleeps like a bird, but I remain
 Like a branch.
I'll say nothing now, I won't disturb its sleep.

26

The cover is torn, and the translator unmasked

By the fire wearing the face of the place.

27

A café—the sea sleeps like a child/

I know this face. 'Hello, how are you?'

I know this voice ...

'The fortune teller hasn't come today ... '

'Is he ill? Has he left?'

   'Strangers dropped him

   In a well ... '

... /the sea sleeps like a child.

28

A bat

   Claims the light is dark,

   And the sun a road to the grave,

Then babbles on.

   The bat didn't fall,

Only the child asleep in dawn's lap fell off.

29

You're not this city or that city
　You're not the sojourn and the memories/the
　　borders are your hostages—your steps are
　　frightened.
The histories of the sky you were
　Are shadows,
　Sparks of a dying flame.

30

A creator devoured by his creatures, a country
　Hiding in the blood running from his remains.
This is the beginning of a new era.

31

Whenever I say: my country is within reach
　And bears fruit in a reachable language
Another language kicks me
To another language.

32

Trees bow to say goodbye

Flowers open, glow, lower their leaves to say
   goodbye,

Roads like pauses between the breathing and
   the words say goodbye,

A body wears sand, falls in a wilderness to say
   goodbye,

The papers that love ink,
   The alphabet, the poets say goodbye,

And the poem says goodbye.

33

All the certainty I have lived slips away

All the torches of my desire slip away

All that was between the faces that lit my exile
   and me slips away

I have to start from the beginning

To teach my limbs to reach the future,

To talk, to climb, to descend from the beginning
In the sky of beginnings, in the abyss of the alphabet.

34

They are falling, the land is a thread of smoke
   Time a train
   Travelling along a track of smoke …
My obsession is here now, loss.
My concern is the end
   Is not over.
They are falling, I am not looking for a new
beginning.

—*Adonis on Beirut, Lebanon*

CITIES OF SOULS &

Broadway

Under Grand Central's tattered vault
   —maybe half a dozen electric stars still lit—
     one saxophone blew, and a sheer black scrim

billowed over some minor constellation
    under repair. Then, on Broadway, red wings
    in a storefront tableau, lustrous, the live macaws

preening, beaks opening and closing
    like those animated knives that unfold all night
    in jewelers' windows. For sale,

glass eyes turned out toward the rain,
    the birds lined up like the endless flowers
    and cheap gems, the makeshift tables

of secondhand magazines
    and shoes the hawkers eye
    while they shelter in the doorways of banks.

So many pockets and paper cups
    and hands reeled over the weight
        of that glittered pavement, and at 103rd

a woman reached to me across the wet roof
    of a stranger's car and said, *I'm Carlotta,*
        I'm hungry. She was only asking for change,

so I don't know why I took her hand.
    The rooftops were glowing above us,
        enormous, crystalline, a second city

lit from within. That night
    a man on the downtown local stood up
        and said, *My name is Ezekiel,*

I am a poet, and my poem this evening is called
    fall. He stood up straight
        to recite, a child reminded of his posture

by the gravity of his text, his hands
hidden in the pockets of his coat.
Love is protected, he said,

the way leaves are packed in snow,
the rubies of fall. God is protecting
the jewel of love for us.

He didn't ask for anything, but I gave him
all the change left in my pocket,
and the man beside me, impulsive, moved,

gave Ezekiel his watch.
It wasn't an expensive watch,
I don't even know if it worked,

but the poet started, then walked away
as if so much good fortune
must be hurried away from,

before anyone realizes it's a mistake.
  Carlotta, her stocking cap glazed
    like feathers in the rain,

under the radiant towers, the floodlit ramparts,
  must have wondered at my impulse to touch her,
    which was like touching myself,

the way your own hand feels when you hold it
  because you want to feel contained.
    She said, *You get home safe now, you hear?*

In the same way Ezekiel turned back
  to the benevolent stranger.
    I will write a poem for you tomorrow,

he said. *The poem I will write will go like this:*
  Our ancestors are replenishing
    the jewel of love for us.

—*Mark Doty on New York City*

An Absolutely
Ordinary Rainbow

The word goes round Repins,
the murmur goes round Lorenzinis,
at Tattersalls, men look up from sheets of numbers,
the Stock Exchange scribblers forget the chalk
  in their hands
and men with bread in their pockets leave the
  Greek Club:
There's a fellow crying in Martin Place.
  They can't stop him.

The traffic in George Street is banked up for
  half a mile
and drained of motion. The crowds are edgy
  with talk
and more crowds come hurrying. Many run in
  the back streets
which minutes ago were busy main streets, pointing:

There's a fellow weeping down there.
　　No one can stop him.
The man we surround, the man no one approaches
simply weeps, and does not cover it, weeps
not like a child, not like the wind, like a man
and does not declaim it, nor beat his breast,
　　nor even
sob very loudly—yet the dignity of his weeping

holds us back from his space, the hollow he
　　makes about him
in the midday light, in his pentagram of sorrow,
and uniforms back in the crowd who tried to
　　seize him
stare out at him, and feel, with amazement,
　　their minds
longing for tears as children for a rainbow.

Some will say, in the years to come, a halo
or force stood around him. There is no such thing.
Some will say they were shocked and would
    have stopped him
but they will not have been there. The fiercest
    manhood,
the toughest reserve, the slickest wit amongst us

trembles with silence, and burns with unexpected
judgements of peace. Some in the concourse
    scream
who thought themselves happy. Only the
    smallest children
and such as look out of Paradise come near him
and sit at his feet, with dogs and dusty pigeons.

Ridiculous, says a man near me, and stops
his mouth with his hands, as if it uttered vomit—

and I see a woman, shining, stretch her hand
and shake as she receives the gift of weeping;
as many as follow her also receive it
and many weep for sheer acceptance, and more
refuse to weep for fear of all acceptance,
but the weeping man, like the earth, requires
   nothing,
the man who weeps ignores us, and cries out
of his writhen face and ordinary body

not words, but grief, not messages, but sorrow,
hard as the earth, sheer, present as the sea —
and when he stops, he simply walks between us
mopping his face with the dignity of one
man who has wept, and now has finished weeping.

Evading believers, he hurries off down Pitt Street.

—*Les Murray on Sydney, Australia*

As My Way Passed Through T'ung-ch'uan, I wished to Visit the Policy Critic of the Right, Mei, But Did Not Know Where To Find Him.

T'ung-ch'uan is a beautiful place:
on all sides, emerald hibiscus!
A tall pagoda guards the pass, alone;
a clear stream embraces city walls.
The marketplace resounds with accents of
    Wu visitors;
some shrines bear dedications from Han days.
I want to visit the Immortal Hermit, Mei,
but which mountain is he hiding on?

—*Tai Piao-yüan on T'ung-ch'uan, China*
[translation by Jonathan Chaves]

Faces in the Street

They lie, the men who tell us in a loud decisive
    tone
That want is here a stranger, and that misery's
    unknown;
For where the nearest suburb and the city
    proper meet
My window-sill is level with the faces in the
    street—
       Drifting past, drifting past,
       To the beat of weary feet—
While I sorrow for the owners of those faces in
    the street.

And cause I have to sorrow, in a land so young
    and fair,
To see upon those faces stamped the marks of
    Want and Care;

I look in vain for traces of the fresh and fair
   and sweet
In sallow, sunken faces that are drifting through
   the street—
     Drifting on, drifting on,
      To the scrape of restless feet;
I can sorrow for the owners of the faces in the street.

In hours before the dawning dims the starlight
in the sky
The wan and weary faces first begin to trickle by,
Increasing as the moments hurry on with
   morning feet,
Till like a pallid river flow the faces in the street—
     Flowing in, flowing in,
      To the beat of hurried feet—
Ah! I sorrow for the owners of those faces in
   the street.

The human river dwindles when 'Tis past the
    hour of eight,
Its waves go flowing faster in the fear of being late;
But slowly drag the moments, whilst beneath
    the dust and heat
The city grinds the owners of the faces in the
    street—
      Grinding body, grinding soul,
      Yielding scarce enough to eat—
Oh! I sorrow for the owners of the faces in the street.

And then the only faces till the sun is sinking down
Are those of outside toilers and the idlers of
    the town,
Save here and there a face that seems a stranger
    in the street,
Tells of the city's unemployed upon his weary
    beat—

Drifting round, drifting round,
To the tread of listless feet—
Ah! My heart aches for the owner of that sad
face in the street.

And when the hours on lagging feet have slowly
dragged away,
And sickly yellow gaslights rise to mock the
going day,
Then flowing past my window like a tide in its
retreat,
Again I see the pallid stream of faces in the
street—
Ebbing out, ebbing out,
To the drag of tired feet,
While my heart is aching dumbly for the faces
in the street.

And now all blurred and smirched with vice the
　　day's sad pages end,
For while the short 'large hours' toward the
　　longer 'small hours' tend,
With smiles that mock the wearer, and with
　　words that half entreat,
Delilah pleads for custom at the corner of the
　　street—
　　　　Sinking down, sinking down,
　　　　Battered wreck by tempests beat—
A dreadful, thankless trade is hers, that Woman
　　of the Street.

But, ah! to dreader things than these our fair
　　young city comes,
For in its heart are growing thick the filthy
　　dens and slums,
Where human forms shall rot away in sties for
　　swine unmeet,

And ghostly faces shall be seen unfit for any street—
   Rotting out, rotting out,
   For the lack of air and meat—
In dens of vice and horror that are hidden from
   the street.

I wonder would the apathy of wealthy men endure
Were all their windows level with the faces of
   the Poor?
Ah! Mammon's slaves, your knees shall knock,
   your hearts in terror beat,
When God demands a reason for the sorrows
   of the street,
     The wrong things and the bad things
     And the sad things that we meet
In the filthy lane and alley, and the cruel,
   heartless street.

I left the dreadful corner where the steps are
    never still,
And sought another window overlooking gorge
    and hill;
But when the night came dreary with the driving
    rain and sleet,
They haunted me—the shadows of those faces
    in the street,
      Flitting by, flitting by,
      Flitting by with noiseless feet,
And with cheeks but little paler than the real
    ones on the street.

Once I cried: 'Oh, God Almighty! if Thy might
    doth still endure,
Now show me in a vision for the wrongs of
    Earth a cure.'

And, lo! with shops all shuttered I beheld a
    city's street,
And in the warning distance heard the tramp
    of many feet,
        Coming near, coming near,
        To a drum's dull distant beat,
And soon I saw the army that was marching
    down the street.

Then, like a swollen river that has broken bank
    and wall,
The human flood came pouring with the red
    flags over all,
And kindled eyes all blazing bright with
    revolutions's heat,
And flashing swords reflecting rigid faces in
    the street.

Pouring on, pouring on,
　　To a drum's loud threatening beat,
And the war-hymns and the cheering of the
　　people in the street.

And so it must be while the world goes rolling
　　round its course,
The warning pen shall write in vain, the
　　warning voice grow hoarse,
But not until a city feels Red Revolution's feet
Shall its sad people miss awhile the terrors of
　　the street—
　　　The dreadful everlasting strife
　　　For scarcely clothes and meat
In that pent track of living death—the city's
　　cruel street.

—*Henry Lawson*

Seoul:
The Uruguay Rounds

I

Banners sway in the air
but the square is emptying.

The girl who was singing
with her arm and fist raised

and pounding the air
above her head like a hammer

rises, dusting off her skirt:
the sun is going down.

Fliers and tracts
unfriendly to the country

from which I have flown
are left behind the leaving

turning to bold-print litter
So what happens now?

Rice will become plentiful
It will become cheaper

lose its flavor
change people.

Your father in North Cholla
may grow ginseng soon

though it will depend
on what others do.

II

Let's walk,
Walk into the streets of neon

lights and choose a place.
The waitress is held

by the evening news.
We seat ourselves

you clear your throat
she takes her time

to notice us then brings us rice
one pot of stew

which we will share
in this nation of friends

though I am not hungry
and wish for you to speak.

Words are grains you keep
from spilling from your mouth.

—*Ann Choi on Seoul, Korea*

Echoes

Traveling at dusk the noisy city street,
I listened to the newsboys' strident cries
Of "Extra," as with flying feet,
They strove to gain this man or that—their prize.
But one was there with neither shout nor stride,
And, having bought from him, I stood nearby,
Pondering the cruel crutches at his side,
Blaming the crowd's neglect, and wondering why—

When suddenly I heard a gruff voice greet
The cripple with "On time to-night?"
Then, as he handed out the sheet,
The Youngster's answer—"You're all right,
My other reg'lars are a little late.
They'll find I'm short one paper when they come;
You see, a strange guy bought one in the wait,
I tho't 'twould cheer him up—he looked so glum!"

So, sheepishly I laughed, and went my way
For I had found a city's heart that day.

—*Ruth Lambert Jones*

The Crowded Street

Let me move slowly through the street,
    Filled with an ever-shifting train,
Amid the sound of steps that beat
    The murmuring walks like autumn rain.

How fast the flitting figures come!
    The mild, the fierce, the stony face;
Some bright with thoughtless smiles, and some
    Where secret tears have left their trace.

They pass—to toil, to strife, to rest;
    To halls in which the feast is spread;
To chambers where the funeral guest
    In silence sits beside the dead.

And some to happy homes repair,
    Where children, pressing cheek to cheek,
With mute caresses shall declare
    The tenderness they cannot speak.

And some, who walk in calmness here,
  Shall shudder as they reach the door
Where one who made their dwelling dear,
  Its flower, its light, is seen no more.

Youth, with pale cheek and slender frame,
  And dreams of greatness in thine eye!
Go'st thou to build an early name,
  Or early in the task to die?

Keen son of trade, with eager brow!
  Who is now fluttering in thy snare?
Thy golden fortunes, tower they now,
  Or melt the glittering spires in air?

Who of this crowd to-night shall tread
  The dance till daylight gleam again?
Who sorrow o'er the untimely dead?
  Who writhe in throes of mortal pain?

Some, famine-struck, shall think how long
   The cold dark hours, how slow the light;
And some, who flaunt amid the throng,
   Shall hide in dens of shame to-night.

Each, where his tasks or pleasures call,
   They pass, and heed each other not.
There is who heeds, who holds them all,
   In His large love and boundless thought.

These struggling tides of life that seem
   In wayward, aimless course to tend,
Are eddies of the mighty stream
   That rolls to its appointed end.

—*William Cullen Bryant*

To —. Composed at Rotterdam.

I gaze upon a city, —
A city new and strange, —
Down many a watery vista
My fancy takes a range;
From side to side I saunter,
And wonder where I am;
And can *you* be in England,
And I at Rotterdam!

Before me lie dark waters
In broad canals and deep
Wheron the silver moonbeams
Sleep, restless in their sleep;
A sort of vulgar Venice
Reminds me where I am;
Yes, yes, you are in England,
And I'm at Rotterdam.

Tall houses with quaint gables,
Where frequent windows shine,
And quays that lead to bridges,
And trees in formal line,
And masts of spicy vessels
From western Surinam,
All tell me you're in England,
But I'm in Rotterdam.

Those sailors, how outlandish
The face and form of each!
They deal in foreign gestures,
And use a foreign speech;
A tongue not learn'd near Isis,
Or studied by the Cam,
Declares that you're in England,
And I'm at Rotterdam.

And now across a market
My doubtful way I trace,
Where stands a solemn statue,
The Genius of the place;
And to the great Erasmus
I offer my salaam;
Who tells me you're in England
But I'm at Rotterdam.

The coffee-room is open—
I mingle in its crowd,—
The dominos are noisy—
The hookahs raise a cloud;
The flavour, none of Fearon's,
That mingles with my dram,
Reminds me you're in England,
And I'm at Rotterdam.

Then here it goes, a bumper—
The toast it shall be mine,
In schiedam, or in sherry,
Tokay, or hock of Rhine;
It well deserves the brightest,
Where sunbeam ever swam—
"The Girl I love in England"
I drink at Rotterdam!

—*Thomas Hood on Rotterdam, The Netherlands*

CITIES AT REST ✑

Port of Spain

Midsummer stretches before me with a cat's yawn.
Trees with dust on their lips, cars melting down
in a furnace. Heat staggers the drifting mongrels.
The capitol has been repainted rose, the rails
round the parks the color of rusting blood;
junta and *coup d'état*, the newest Latino mood,
broods on the balcony. Monotonous lurid bushes
brush the damp air with the ideograms of buzzards
over the Chinese groceries. The oven alleys stifle
where mournful tailors peer over old machines
stitching June and July together seamlessly,
and one waits for lightning as the armed sentry
hopes in boredom for the crack of a rifle—
but I feed on its dust, its ordinariness,
on the inertia that fills its exiles with horror,
on the dust over the hills with their orange lights,
even on the pilot light in the reeking harbor
that turns like a police car's. The terror

is local, at least. Like the magnolia's whorish whiff.
And the dog barks of the revolution crying wolf.
The moon shines like a lost button;
the black water stinks under the sodium lights on
the wharf. The night is turned on as firmly
as a switch, dishes clatter behind bright windows,
I walk along the walls with occasional shadows
that say nothing. Sometimes, in narrow doors
there are old men playing the same quiet games—
cards, draughts, dominoes. I give them names.
The night is companionable, the day is so fierce as
our human future anywhere. I can understand
Borges's blind love of Buenos Aires,
how a man feels the veins of a city swell in his hand.

—*Derek Walcott on Port-of-Spain, Trinidad*

Evocation of Recife

Recife
Not the American Venice,
or the Mauritsstad of the speculators of the
  Dutch East India
                                    Company
nor the Recife of Portuguese traders
nor even the Recife I learned in time to love—
  The Recife of revolutionaries and leftists
but a Recife without history or literature,
Recife without anything else
The Recife of my childhood.

Union Street where I played crack-the-whip
  and smashed
    Windows in the house of Dona Aninha Viega
Tôtonio Rodrigues was very old and wore a
  pince-nez at the end
                                    of his nose

After dinner, the families took chairs out onto
   the sidewalk,

                      gossiping, flirting, laughing
We played in the street.
The boys called out
   Run rabbit!
   Don't run!

In the distance, the voices of the little girls
were softer:
   Rosebush give me a flower,
   Carnation, give me a bud

(And of all those roses,
how many died in the bud?)

Suddenly,
   in the distances of the night

                           a bell

One grown-up person said:

"A fire in Santo Antonio!"

Another contradicted: "São José!"

Tôtonio Rodrigues always thought it was São José.

The men clapped on their hats and went off,
    smoking,

and I hated being a kid because I couldn't tag
    along to see the fire.

Union Street...

The streets of my boyhood had such great
names!

Sun Street.

(I hate to think it might have been renamed for
    some bigwig, the

                    Boulevard of Dr. Fulano de Tal.)

Behind our house was Nostalgia Street...

                ...where we used to go and smoke.

On the other side was the wharf on Dawn Street,
                ...where we used to sneak off to fish.

Capiberibe.
  Capibarebe

Then, way in the distance, there were the fields
  of Caxangá
and its straw bathhouses

One day I saw a girl altogether naked in her bath.
I froze, my heart pounding,
She laughed.
  It was my first epiphany

Floods! The floods! Mud dead on ox trees debris,
  whirlpools—all

                                                    gone
And between the pillars of the railroad bridge,
  heroes
    Maneuvering their rafts of banana logs.
Novenas
  Cavalhadas

My head was in the girl's lap, and she was
running her fingers

                              through my hair

Capiperibe
- Capibaribe

On Union Street, every afternoon, the woman
   who sold bananas
     came around in her bright rough shawl
and the peddler of sugar cane
and the peanut vendor
   we called them beenuts and they weren't
   roasted but boiled

I remember all the hawkers' cries:
   Eggs fresh and cheap
   Ten eggs for a pataca

Life wasn't filtered through newspapers or books
But came from the mouth of the people, the
    flawed speech of the
        people
the correct speech of the people
because the people speak Brazilian Portuguese
    with gusto
        beating us by a mile
        because all we can do
        is stammer and parrot
        the old syntax of *The Lusiads*.
Life with its serving of sweets I couldn't begin
    to understand
Territory I had not yet started to map

Recife...
    Union Street
        My grandfather's house...
I never supposed that house could disappear.

Everything there looked to me to be eternal
Recife...
   My grandfather, dead.
Dead Recife, wonderful Recife, Recife as Brazilian
   as my
                      grandfather's house.

—Antonio Manuel Bandeira on Recife, Brazil.

A Ballade of Home

Let others prate of Greece and Rome,
　And towns where they may never be,
The muse should wander nearer home.
　My country is enough for me;
　Her wooded hills that watch the sea,
Her inland miles of springing corn,
　At Macedon or Barrakee—
I love the land where I was born.

On Juliet smile the autumn stars
　And windswept plains by Winchelsea,
In summer on their sandy bars
　Her rivers loiter languidly.
　Where singing waters fall and flee
The gullied ranges dip to Lorne
　With musk and gum and myrtle tree—
I love the land where I was born.

The wild things in her tangles move
    As blithe as fauns in Sicily,
Where Melbourne rises roof by roof
    The tall ships serve her at the quay,
    And hers the yoke of liberty
On stalwart shoulders lightly worn,
    Where thought and speech and prayer are free—
I love the land where I was born.

Princes and lords of high degree,
    Smile, and we fling you scorn for scorn,
In hope and faith and memory
    I love the land where I was born.

—*Enid Derham on Melbourne, Australia*

Ottawa

City about whose brow the north winds blow,
Girdled with woods and shod with river foam,
Called by a name as old as Troy or Rome,
Be great as they but pure as thine own snow;
Rather flash up amid the auroral glow,
The Lamia city of the northern star,
Than be so hard with craft or wild with war,
Peopled with deeds remembered for their woe.
Thou art too bright for guile, too young for tears,
And thou wilt live to be too strong for Time;
For he may mock thee with his furrowed frowns,
But thou wilt grow in calm throughout the years,
Cinctured with peace and crowned with power
    sublime,
The maiden queen of all the towered towns.

—*Duncan Campbell Scott on Ottawa, Canada*

Upon Westminster Bridge

Earth has not anything to show more fair:
Dull would he be of soul who could pass by
A sight so touching in its majesty:
This City now doth like a garment wear
The beauty of the morning; silent, bare,
Ships, towers, domes, theatres, and temples lie
Open unto the fields, and to the sky;
All bright and glittering in the smokeless air.
Never did sun more beautifully steep
In his first splendour, valley rock or hill;
Ne'er saw I, never felt, a calm so deep!
The river glideth at his own sweet will:
Dear God! the very houses seem asleep;
And all that mighty heart is lying still!

—*William Wordsworth on London, England*

San Ildefonso* Nocturne

1
In my window night

invents another night
another space:

carnival convulsed
In a square yard of blackness.

Momentary
confederations of fire,

nomadic geometries,
errant numbers.

From yellow to green to red,
the spiral unwinds.

Window:
magnetic plate of calls and answers,
high-voltage calligraphy,
false heaven/hell of industry
on the changing skin of the moment.

*College in Mexico City, established in 1559 by Jesuits. Now site of modern art museum.

Sign-seeds:
          the night shoots them off,
they rise,
        bursting above,
               fall
still burning
        in a cone of shadow,
                   reappear,
rambling sparks,
        syllable-clusters,
spinning flames
        that scatter,
                smithereens once more.
The city invents and erases them.

I am at the entrance to a tunnel.
These phrases drill through time.
Perhaps I am that which waits at the end of the
    tunnel.

I speak with eyes closed.

                              Someone

has planted

               a forest of magnetic needles

in my eyelids,

                someone

guides the thread of these words.

                            The page

has become an ants' nest.

                    The void

has settled at the pit of my stomach.

                              I fall

endlessly through that void.

                     I fall without falling.

My hands are cold,

                my feet cold—

but the alphabets are burning, burning.

                            Space

makes and unmakes itself.

The night insists,
the night touches my forehead,
touches my thoughts.
What does it want?

2

Empty streets, squinting lights.
On a corner,
the ghost of a dog
searches the garbage
for a spectral bone.
Uproar in a nearby patio:
cacophonous cockpit.
Mexico, circa 1931.
Loitering sparrows,
a flock of children
builds a nest
of unsold newspapers.

In the desolation
              the streetlights invent
unreal pools of yellowish light.
                    Apparitions:
time splits open:
              a lugubrious, lascivious clatter of heels,
beneath *a sky of soot*
                    the flash of a skirt.
C'est la mort—ou la morte . . .
                    The indifferent wind
rips posters from the walls.

At this hour,
              the red walls of San Ildefonso
are black, and they breathe:
                    sun turned to time,
time turned to stone,
                    stone turned to body.

These streets were once canals.

                             In the sun,

the houses were silver:

                             city of mortar and stone,

moon fallen in the lake.

                          Over the filled canals

and the buried idols

                    the *criollos* erected

another city

                —not white, but red and gold—

idea turned to space, tangible number.

                        They placed it

at the crossroads of eight directions,

                          its doors

open to the invisible:

                    heaven and hell.

Sleeping district.

                 We walk through galleries of echoes,

past broken images:

                our history.

Hushed nation of stones.

                       Churches

dome-growths,

              their facades

petrified gardens of symbols.

                     Shipwrecked

in the spiteful proliferation of dwarf houses:

humiliated palaces,

               fountains without water,

affronted frontispieces.

                  Cumuli,

insubstantial madrepore,

                    accumulate

over the ponderous bulks,

                   conquered

not by the weight of the years

but by the infamy of the present.

Zócalo Plaza*,
vast as the heavens:
diaphanous space,
court of echoes.
There,
with Alyosha K and Julien S,
we devised bolts of lightning
against the century and its cliques.
The wind of thought
carried us away,
the verbal wind,
the wind that plays with mirrors,
master of reflections,
builder of cities of air,
geometries
hung from the thread of reason.

*square in central Mexico City, and focal point of cultural and
national importance. Site of celebrations and political protests.

Shut down for the night,

                        the yellow trolleys,

giant worms.

               S's and Z's:

a crazed auto, insect with malicious eyes.

                            Ideas,

fruits within an arm's reach,

                   like stars,

                       burning.

The girandola is burning,

                the adolescent dialogue,

the scorched hasty frame.

             The bronze fist

of the towers beats

          12 times.

              Night

bursts into pieces,

> gathers them by itself,
and becomes one, intact.
> > We disperse,
not there in the plaza with its dead trains,
> > > but here,
on this page: petrified letters.

3

The boy who walks through this poem,
between San Ildefonso and the Zócalo,
is the man who writes it:
> > this page too
is a ramble through the night.
> > > Here the friendly ghosts
become flesh,
> > ideas dissolve.

Good, we wanted good:
> > to set the world right.

We didn't lack integrity:

                    we lacked humility.

What we wanted was not innocently wanted.

Precepts and concepts,

                    the arrogance of theologians,

to beat with a cross,

                    to institute with blood,

to build the house with bricks of crime,

to declare obligatory communion.

                              Some

became secretaries to the secretary

to the General Secretary of the Inferno.

                              Rage

became philosophy,

                    its drivel has covered the planet.

Reason came down to earth,

took the form of a gallows

                    —and is worshipped by millions.

Circular plot:

we have all been,
in the Grand Theater of Filth,
judge, executioner, victim, witness,

we have all
given false testimony
against the others
and against ourselves.

And the most vile: we
were the public that applauded or yawned in its seats.
The guilt that knows no guilt,
innocence
was the greatest guilt.

Each year was a mountain of bones.

Conversions, retractions, excommunications,
reconciliations, apostasies, recantations,
the zigzag of the demonolatries and the
androlatries,

bewitchments and aberrations:
my history.
        Are they the histories of an error?
History is the error.
        Beyond dates,
before names,
        truth is that
which history scorns:
        the everyday
—everyone's anonymous heartbeat,
        the unique
beat of every one—
        the unrepeatable
everyday, identical to all days.
        Truth
is the base of a time without history.
        The weight
of the weightless moment:
        a few stones in the sun

seen long ago,

         today return,

stones of time that are also stone

beneath this sun of time,

sun that comes from a dateless day,

                 sun

that lights up these words,

           sun of words

that burns out when they are named.

            Suns, words, stones,

burn and burn out:

        the moment burns them

without burning.

       Hidden, unmoving, untouchable,

the present—not its presences—is always.

Between seeing and making,

         contemplation or action,

I chose the act of words:

            to make them, to inhabit them,
to give eyes to the language.
                    Poetry is not truth:
it is the resurrection of presences,
                         history
transfigured in the truth of undated time.
Poetry,
    like history, is made;
                 poetry,
like truth, is seen.
            Poetry:
                  incarnation
of the-sun-on-the-stones in a name,
                      dissolution
of the name in a beyond of stones.
Poetry,
    suspension bridge between history and truth,
is not a path toward this or that:
                  it is to see

the stillness in motion,

                    change

in stillness.

            History is the path:

it goes nowhere,

                we all walk it,

truth is to walk it.

                  We neither go nor come:

we are in the hands of time.

                    Truth:

to know ourselves,

                from the beginning,

                        hung.

Brotherhood over the void.

4

Ideas scatter,

            the ghosts remain:

truth of the lived and suffered.
An almost empty taste remains:

                              time
—shared fury—
                  time
—shared oblivion—

                        in the end transfigured
in memory and its incarnations.

                              What remains is
time as portioned body: language.

In the window,

                  travesties of battle:
the commercial sky of advertisements

                              flares up, goes out.
Behind,

            barely visible,

                        the true constellations.

Among the water towers, antennas, rooftops,
a liquid column,
                    more mental than corporeal,
a waterfall of silence:
                    the moon.
                         Neither phantom nor idea:
once a goddess,
                    today an errant clarity.

My wife sleeps.
                    She too is a moon,
A clarity that travels
                    not between the reefs of the clouds,
but between the rocks and wracks of dreams:
she too is a soul.
                    She flows below her closed eyes,
a silent torrent
                    rushing down

from her forehead to her feet,

                                 she tumbles within,

bursts out from within,

                             her heartbeats sculpt her,

traveling through herself,

                             she invents herself,

inventing herself

                   she copies it,

she is an arm of the sea

                      between the islands of her breasts,

her belly a lagoon

                        where darkness and its foliage

grow pale,

                   she flows through her shape,

rises,

         falls,

                scatters in herself,

                          ties

herself to her flowing,

                disperses in her form:

she too is a body.

            Truth

is the swell of a breath

and the visions closed eyes see:

the palpable mystery of the person.

The night is at the point of running over.

                  It grows light.

The horizon has become aquatic.

                 To rush down

from the heights of this hour:

              will dying

be a falling or a rising,

          a sensation or a cessation?

I close my eyes,

        I hear in my skull

the footsteps of my blood,

                    I hear

time pass through my temples.

                            I am still alive.

The room is covered with moon.

                         Woman:

fountain in the night.

                    I am bound to her quiet flowing.

—*Octavio Paz on Mexico City, Mexico*

To Sydney

City, I never told you yet—
   O little City, let me tell—
A secret woven of your wiles,
   Dear City with the angel face,
   And you will hear with frowning grace,
Or will you break in summer smiles?

This is the secret, little town
   Lying so lightly towards the sea;
City, my secret has no art,
   Dear City with the golden door;
   But oh, the whispers I would pour
Into your ears—into your heart!

You are my lover, little place,
   Lying so sweetly all alone.
And yet I cannot, cannot tell
   My secret, for the voice will break
   That tries to tell of all the ache
Of this poor heart beneath your spell.

Dreaming, I tell you all my tale;
   Tell how the tides that wash your feet
Sink through my heart and cut its cords.
   Dreaming, I hold my arms and drag
   All, all into my heart—the flag
On the low hill turned harbourwards,

And all the curving little bays,
   The hot, dust-ridden, narrow streets,
The languid turquoise of the sky,
   The gardens flowing to the wave,
   I drag them in. O City, save
The grave for me where I must lie.

Yet humbly I would try to build
   Stone upon stone for this town's sake;
 Humbly would try for you to aid
   Those whose wise love for you will rear
   White monuments far off and near,
White, but unsoiled, undesecrate.

—*Louise Mack on Sydney, Australia*

VENICE

Venice, thou Siren of sea-cities, wrought
By mirage, built on water, stair o'er stair,
Of sunbeams and cloud-shadows, phantom-fair,
With naught of earth to mar thy sea-born thought!
Thou floating film upon the wonder-fraught
Ocean of dreams! Thou hast no dream so rare
As are thy sons and daughters, they who wear
Foam-flakes of charm from thine enchantment
  caught!
O dark brown eyes! O tangles of dark hair!
O heaven-blue eyes, blonde tresses where the breeze
Plays over sun-burn'd cheeks in sea-blown air!
Firm limbs of molded bronze! frank debonair
Smiles of deep-bosom'd women! Loves that seize
Man's soul, and waft her on storm-melodies!

—*John Addington Symonds on Venice, Italy*

CITIES IN THE PAST ❧

The Aztec City

There is a clouded city, gone to rest
   Beyond the crest
Where cordilleras mar the mystic west.

There suns unheeded rise and re-arise;
   And in the skies
The harvest moon unnoticed lives and dies.

And yet this clouded city has no night—
   Volcanic light
Compels eternal noontide, redly bright.

A thousand wells, whence cooling waters came,
   No more the same,
Now send aloft a thousand jets of flame.

This clouded city is enchanting fair,
   For rich and rare
From sculptured frieze the gilded griffins stare.

With level look—with loving, hopeful face,
    Fixed upon space,
Stand caryatides of unknown race,

And colonnades of dark green serpentine,
    Of strange design,
Carved on whose shafts queer alphabets combine.

And there are lofty temples, rich and great,
    And at the gate,
Carved in obsidian, the lions wait.

And from triumphant arches, looking down
    Upon the town,
In porphyry, sad, unknown statesmen frown.

And there are palace homes, and stately walls,
    And open halls
Where fountains are, with voiceless water-falls.

The ruddy fire incessantly illumes
    Temples and tombs,
And in its blaze the stone-wrought cactus blooms.

From clouds congealed the mercury distils,
    And, forming rills,
Adown the streets in double streamlet trills.

As rains from clouds, that summer skies eclipse,
    From turret-tips
And spire and porch the mobile metal drips.

No one that visited this fiery hive
    Ever alive
Came out but me—I, I alone, survive.

—*Eugene Fitch Ware ("Ironquill")*

Nuremburg

In the valley of the Pegnitz, where across broad
  meadowlands
Rise the blue Franconian mountains, Nuremburg,
  the ancient, stands.

Quaint old town of toil and traffic, quaint old
  town of art and song,
Memories haunt thy pointed gables, like the
  rooks that round them throng:

Memories of the Middle Ages, when the
  emperors, rough and bold,
Had their dwelling in thy castle, time-defying,
  centuries old;

And thy brave and thrifty burghers boasted,
  in their uncouth rhyme,
That their great imperial city stretched its hand
  through every clime.

In the court-yard of the castle, bound with
many an iron band,
Stands the mighty linden planted by Queen
Cunigunde's hand;

On the square the oriel window, where in old
heroic days
Sat the poet Melchior singing Kaiser Maximilian's
praise.

Everywhere I see around me rise the wondrous
world of Art:
Fountains wrought with richest sculpture
standing in the common mart;

And above cathedral doorways saints and
bishops carved in stone,
By a former age commissioned as apostles to
our own.

In the church of sainted Sebald sleeps
   enshrined his holy dust,
And in bronze the Twelve Apostles guard from
   age to age their trust;

In the church of sainted Lawrence stands a pix
   of sculpture rare,
Like the foamy sheaf of fountains, rising
   through the painted air.

Here, when Art was still religion, with a simple,
   reverent heart,
Lived and labored Albrecht Dürer, the Evangelist
   of Art;

Hence in silence and in sorrow, toiling still with
   busy hand,
Like an emigrant he wandered, seeking for the
   Better Land.

Emigravit is the inscription on the tombstone
    where he lies;
Dead he is not, but departed,—for the artist
    never dies.

Fairer seems the ancient city, and the sunshine
    seems more fair,
That he once has trod its pavement, that he
    once has breathed its air!

Through these streets so broad and stately,
    these obscure and dismal lanes,
Walked of yore the Mastersingers, chanting
    rude poetic strains.

From remote and sunless suburbs came they to
    the friendly guild,
Building nests in Fame's great temple, as in
    spouts the swallows build.

As the weaver plied the shuttle, wove he too the
    mystic rhyme,
And the smith his iron measures hammered to
    the anvil's chime;

Thanking God, whose boundless wisdom makes
    the flowers of poesy bloom
In the forge's dust and cinders, in the tissues of
    the loom.

Here Hans Sachs, the cobbler-poet, laureate of
    the gentle craft,
Wisest of the Twelve Wise Masters, in huge
    folios sang and laughed.

But his house is now an ale-house, with a nicely
    sanded floor,
And a garland in the window, and his face above
    the door;

Painted by some humble artist, as in Adam
  Puschman's song,
As the old man gray and dove-like, with his
  great beard white and long.

And at night the swart mechanic comes to
  drown his cark and care,
Quaffing ale from pewter tankards, in the
  master's antique chair.

Vanished is the ancient splendor, and before my
  dreamy eye
Wave these mingled shapes and figures, like a
  faded tapestry.

Not thy Councils, not thy Kaisers, win for thee
    the world's regard;
But thy painters Albrecht Dürer, and Hans
    Sachs, thy cobbler bard.

Thus, O Nuremberg, a wanderer from a region
    far away,
As he paced thy streets and court-yards, sang
    in thought his careless lay:

Gathering from the pavement's crevice, as a
    floweret of the soil,
The nobility of labor—the long pedigree of toil.

—*Henry Wadsworth Longfellow on Nuremberg, Germany*

Rome: Building a New Street in the Ancient Quarter (April, 1887)

These numbered cliffs and gnarls of masonry
Outskeleton Time's central city, Rome;
Whereof each arch, entablature, and dome
Lies bare in all its gaunt anatomy.

And cracking frieze and rotten metope
Express, as though they were an open tome
Top-lined with caustic monitory gnome;
"Dunces, Learn here to spell Humanity!"

And yet within these ruins' very shade
The singing workmen shape and set and join
Their frail new mansion's stuccoed cove and quoin
With no apparent sense that years abrade,
Though each rent wall their feeble works invade
Once shamed all such in power of pier and groin.

—*Thomas Hardy on Rome, Italy*

Duns Scotus's Oxford

Towery city and branchy between towers;
Cuckoo-echoing, bell-swarmèd, lark-charmèd,
    rook-racked, river-rounded;
The dapple-eared lily below thee; that country
    and town did
Once encounter in, here coped and poisèd powers;

Thou hast a base and brickish skirt there, sours
That neighbour-nature thy grey beauty is
    grounded
Best in; graceless growth, thou hast confounded
Rural rural keeping—folk, flocks, and flowers.

Yet ah! this air I gather and I release
He lived on; these weeds and waters, these
    walls are what
He haunted who of all men most sways my
spirits to peace;

Of realty the rarest-veinèd unraveller; a not
Rivalled insight, be rival Italy or Greece;
Who fired France for Mary without spot.

—*Gerard Manley Hopkins on Oxford, England*

Philadelphia

If you're off to Philadelphia in the morning,
You mustn't take my stories for a guide.
There's little left, indeed, of the city you will
    read of,
And all the folk I write about have died.
Now few will understand if you mention
    Talleyrand,
Or remember what his cunning and his skill did;
And the cabmen at the wharf do not know
    Count Zinzendorf,
Nor the Church in Philadelphia he builded.

It is gone, gone, gone with lost Atlantis,
(Never say I didn't give you warning).
In Seventeen Ninety-three 'twas there for all
    to see,
But it's not in Philadelphia this morning.

If you're off to Philadelphia in the morning,
You mustn't go by anything I've said.
Bob Bicknell's Southern Stages have been laid
aside for ages,
But the Limited will take you there instead.
Toby Hirte can't be seen at One Hundred and
Eighteen
North Second Street—no matter when you call;
And I fear you'll search in vain for the wash-
house down the lane
Where Pharaoh played the fiddle at the ball.

It is gone, gone, gone with Thebes the Golden,
(Never say I didn't give you warning).
In Seventeen Ninety-four 'twas a famous
dancing floor—
But it's not in Philadelphia this morning.

If you're off to Philadelphia in the morning,
You must telegraph for rooms at some Hotel.
You needn't try your luck at Epply's or "The Buck,"
Though the Father of his Country liked them well.
It is not the slightest use to inquire for Adam Goos,
Or to ask where Pastor Meder has removed—so
You must treat as out of date the story I relate
Of the Church in Philadelphia he loved so.

He is gone, gone, gone with Martin Luther
(Never say I didn't give you warning)
In Seventeen Ninety-five he was, (rest his soul!)
    alive.
But he's not in Philadelphia this morning.

If you're off to Philadelphia this morning,
And wish to prove the truth of what I say,
I pledge my word you'll find the pleasant land behind

Unaltered since Red Jacket rod that way.

Still the pine-woods scent the noon; still the
catbird sings his tune;

Still autumn sets the maple-forest blazing;

Still the grape-vine through the dusk flings her
soul-compelling musk;

Still the fire-flies in the corn make night amazing!

They are there, there, there with Earth immortal

(Citizens, I give you friendly warning)

The things that truly last when men and times
have passed,

They are all in Pennsylvania this morning!

—*Rudyard Kipling on Philadelphia, Pennsylvania*

DUBLIN

Grey brick upon brick,
Declamatory bronze
On somber pedestals—
O'Connell, Grattan, Moore—
And the brewery tugs and the swans
On the balustraded stream
And the bare bones of a fanlight
Over a hungry door
And the air soft on the cheek
And porter running from the taps
With a head of yellow cream
And Nelson on his pillar
Watching his world collapse.

This was never my town,
I was not born nor bred
Nor schooled here and she will not
Have me alive or dead

But yet she holds my mind
With her seedy elegance,
With her gentle veils of rain
And all her ghosts that walk
And all that hide behind
Her Georgian façades—
The catcalls and the pain,
The glamour of her squalor,
The bravado of her talk.

The lights jig in the river
With a concertina movement
And the sun comes up in the morning
Like barley-sugar on the water
And the mist on the Wicklow hills
Is close, as close
As the peasantry were to the landlord,
As the Irish to the Anglo-Irish,

As the killer is close one moment
To the man he kills,
Or as the moment itself
Is close to the next moment.

She is not an Irish town
And she is not English,
Historic with guns and vermin
And the cold renown
Of a fragment of Church latin,
Of an oratorical phrase.
But oh the days are soft,
Soft enough to forget
The lesson better learnt,
The bullet on the wet
Streets, the crooked deal,
The steel behind the laugh,
The Four Courts burnt.

Fort of the Dane,
Garrison of the Saxon,
Augustan capital
Of a Gaelic nation,
Appropriating all
The alien brought,
You give me time for thought
And by a juggler's trick
You poise the toppling hour—
O greyness run to flower,
Grey stone, grey water,
And brick upon grey brick.

—*Louis MacNeice on Dublin, Ireland*

Buenos Aires

In my room at the Hotel Continental
a thousand miles from nowhere,
I heard
The bulky, beefy breathing of the herds.

Cattle furnished my new clothes:
my coat of limp, chestnut-colored suede,
my sharp shoes
that hurt my toes.

A false fin-de-siècle decorum
snored over Buenos Aires,
lost in the pampas
and run by the barracks.
Old strong men denied apotheosis,
bankrupt, on horseback, welded to their horses, moved
white marble rearing moon-shaped hooves,
to strike the country down.

Romantic military sculpture
waved sabers over Dickensian architecture,
laconic squads patrolled the blanks
left by the invisible poor.

All day I read about newspaper *coup d'états*
of the leaden, internecine generals—
lumps of dough on the chessboard—and never saw
their countermarching tanks.

Along the sunlit cypress walks
Of the Republican Martyrs' graveyard,
Hundreds of one-room Roman temples
hugged their neo-classical catafalques.

Literal commemorative busts
preserved the frogged coats
and fussy, furrowed foreheads
of those soldier bureaucrats.

By their brazen doors
a hundred marble goddesses
wept like willows. I found rest
by cupping a soft palm to each hard breast.

That night I walked the streets.
My pinched feet bled in my shoes. In a park
I fought off seduction from the dark
python bodies of new world demigods.

Everywhere, the bellowing of the old bull—
the muzzled underdogs still roared
for the brute beef of Peron,
the nymphets' Don Giovanni.

On the main square
a white stone obelisk
rose like a phallus
without flesh or hair—

always my lighthouse
homeward to the hotel!
My breath whitened the winter air,
I was the worse for wear.

When the night's blackness spilled,
I saw the light of morning
on Buenos Aires filled
with frowning, starch-collared crowds.

—*Robert Lowell on Buenos Aires, Argentina*

Mannahatta

I was asking for something specific and perfect
    for my city,
Whereupon lo! upsprang the aboriginal name.

Now I see what there is in a name, a work,
    liquid, sane, unruly, musical, self-sufficient,
I see that the word of my city is that word from
    of old,
Because I see that word nested in nests of
    water-bays, superb,
Rich, hemm'd thick all around with sailships
    and steamships, an island sixteen miles long,
    solid-founded,
Numberless crowded streets, high growths of
    iron, slender, strong, light, splendidly
    uprising toward clear skies,
Tides swift and ample, well-loved by me,
    toward sundown,

The flowing sea-currents, the little islands,
    larger adjoining islands, the heights, the villas,
The countless masts, the white shore-steamers,
    the lighters, the ferry-boats, the black sea-
    steamers well-model'd,
The down-town streets, the jobbers' houses of
    business, the houses of business of the ship-
    merchants and money-brokers, the river-streets,
Immigrants arriving, fifteen or twenty thousand
    in a week,
The carts hauling goods, the manly race of
    drivers of horses, the brown-faced sailors,
The summer air, the bright sun shining, and
    the sailing clouds aloft,
The winter snows, the sleigh-bells, the broken
    ice in the river, passing along up or down
    with the flood tide or ebb-tide,

The mechanics of the city, the masters, well-
    form'd, beautiful-faced, looking you straight
    in the eyes,
Trottoirs throng'd, vehicles, Broadway, the
    women, the shops and shows,
A million people—manners free and superb—
    open voices—hospitality—the most courageous
    and friendly young men,
City of hurried and sparkling waters! city of
    spires and masts!
City nested in bays! my city!

—*Walt Whitman on New York City*

On the Building
of Springfield

Let not our town be large—remembering
  That little Athens was the Muses' home;
That Oxford rules the heart of London still,
  That Florence gave the Renaissance to Rome.

Record it for the grandson of your son—
  A city is not builded in a day:
Our little town cannot complete her soul
  Till countless generations pass away.

Now let each child be joined as to a church
  To her perpetual hopes, each man ordained;
Let every street be made a reverent aisle
  Where music grows, and beauty is unchained.

Let Science and Machinery and Trade
   Be slaves of her, and make her all in all—
Building against our blatant restless time
   An unseen, skillful, medieval wall.

Let every citizen be rich toward God.
   Let Christ, the beggar, teach divinity—
Let no man rule who holds his money dear.
   Let this, our city, be our luxury.

We should build parks that students from afar
   Would choose to starve in, rather than go home—
Fair little squares, with Phidian ornament—
   Food for the spirit, milk and honeycomb.

Songs shall be sung by us in that good day—
  Songs we have written—blood within the rhyme
Beating, as when old England still was glad,
  The purple, rich, Elizabethan time.

Say, is my prophecy too fair and far?
  I only know, unless her faith be high,
The soul of this our Nineveh is doomed,
  Our little Babylon will surely die.

Some city on the breast of Illinois
  No wiser and no better at the start,
By faith shall rise redeemed—by faith shall rise
  Bearing the western glory in her heart—

The genius of the Maple, Elm and Oak,
  The secret hidden in each grain of corn—
The glory that the prairie angels sing
  At night when sons of Life and Love are born—

Born but to struggle, squalid and alone,
  Broken and wandering in their early years.
When will they make our dusty streets their goal,
  Within our attics hide their sacred tears?

When will they start our vulgar blood athrill
  With living language—words that set us free?
When will they make a path of beauty clear
  Between our riches and our liberty?

We must have many Lincoln-hearted men—
  A city is not builded in a day—
And they must do their work, and come and go
  While countless generations pass away.

—*Vachel Lindsay on Springfield, Illinois*

Washington

The white-walled Rome of an unwritten epic,
  Spreading like the waters of a new well run;
Drinking at the lips of a clear green river
  Rising in the fountains and the wells of the sun!

Nothing of imperial dust in her cellars,
  Nothing of the torn old tower and dome;
Mistress of her clean white halls unhaunted—
  City of the sunrise, altar, and home!

City of the sunrise hills unhaunted
  By the skulls of kings and the ribs of decay;
Seeded in the earth like a clean deep tap-root—
  The granite in the oak of her boughs today!
A white ship built in a cool green forest
  And launched with the green leaves fresh on
    her bow,

Sun on her sails and foam on her anchors,
  Halfway out on her maiden trip now!

The clean new Rome of an unwritten epic,
  Spreading to the borders of a universal dream;
A white ship launched on a universal river,
  Steering for the sun at the mouth of the stream!

—*Aloysius Coll on Washington, D.C.*

The Place of the Damned

All folks who pretend to religion and grace,
Allow there's a Hell, but dispute of the place:
But, if Hell may by logical rules be defined
The place of the damned—I'll tell you my mind.
Wherever the damned do chiefly abound,
Most certainly there is Hell to be found:
Damned poets, damned critics, damned
    blockheads, damned knaves,
Damned senators bribed, damned prostitute
    slaves;
Damned lawyers and judges, damned lords and
    damned squires;
Damned spies and informers, damned friends
    and damned liars;
Damned villains, corrupted in every station;
Damned time-serving priests all over the nation
And into the bargain I'll readily give you
Damned ignorant prelates, and counsellors privy.

Then let us no longer by parsons be flammed,

For we know by these marks the place of the
damned:

And hell to be sure is at Paris or Rome.

How happy for us that it is not at home!

—*Jonathan Swift*

MODERN CITIES ⁊

Eiffel Tower

To Robert Delaunay

Eiffel Tower
Guitar of the sky
    Your wireless telegraphy
    Attracts words
    As a rosebush the bees
During the night
The Seine no longer flows

    Telescope or bugle

    EIFFEL TOWER

And it's a hive of words
Or an inkwell of honey

At the bottom of dawn
A spider with barbed-wire legs
Was making its web of clouds

My little boy
To climb the Eiffel Tower
You climb on a song

    Do

      re

        mi

          fa

            sol

              la

                ti

                  do

We are up on top

A bird sings   It's the wind
in the telegraph Of Europe
antennae   The electric wind
  Over there

The hats fly away
They have wings but they don't sing

Jacqueline
    Daughter of France
What do you see up there

The Seine is asleep
Under the shadow of its bridges

I see the Earth turning
And I blow my bugle
Toward all the seas

    On the path
    Of your perfume
    All the bees and the words go their way

On the four horizons
Who has not heard this song

I AM THE QUEEN OF THE DAWN OF
    THE POLES
I AM THE COMPASS THE ROSE OF THE
    WINDS THAT FADES EVERY FALL
AND ALL FULL OF SNOW
I DIE FROM THE DEATH OF THAT ROSE
IN MY HEAD A BIRD SINGS ALL YEAR
    LONG

That's the way the Tower spoke to me one day

Eiffel Tower
    Aviary of the world
        Sing   Sing
Chimes of Paris

The giant hanging in the midst of the void
Is the poster of France

    The day of Victory
    You will tell it to the stars

—*Vicente Huidobro on Paris, France*

Spring's Brief Visit to Taipei

When spring paid Taipei a brief visit
She ambled over, sneaking through the city gates
At that time Taipei had no window grates
    So spring would often beckon at the windows
        of each home
    Would help the young roadside grass to
        straighten up
    Tell each flower to open its mouth only after
        brushing its teeth
    And never let itself convey the least bit of filth

    Those days, Taipei didn't have too many tall
        buildings
    So spring didn't have to climb too high
    Those days, Taipei didn't have too many
        water faucets
    So spring often went into the Tamkang River
        to wash her hands

Those days, early morning was a time for
   gymnastics in Taipei
So when spring sauntered out, she had no
   need of a face mask
Those days, Taipei didn't have many motor
   engines
So spring wasn't startled by a sudden noise
Those days, zebra-striped crosswalks were
   enough to stop traffic
So spring was not afraid to be turned topsy-
   turvy by the wind
Those days, spring wouldn't miss traffic
   signs, even if she had to wear glasses

You didn't need to drive a car to be honked
   off by a horn
Nor worry about dumping garbage and being
   fined by the EPA

Those days, yawping spring would often wear
     miniskirts
For everyone to see, and people would start
     whistling
Those days …
Those days, you wouldn't find spring sleeping
     in the public park
   Nor parking on the road dividers
   Nor squatting on flower pots, to "fertilize" them
   Nor going up and down in an all-glass elevator
Those days, spring wouldn't climb over the walls
   No need to see one's own name upside down
     on the shutter
   No need to beckon children through a keyhole
   No need to put on a TV show for every
     household

Spring—ah!—Spring came to Taipei for only a
    brief visit
And then she left
She's an old hag now, walking all this time on
    bound feet
She said, if she walks any slower, she might be
    crushed by a mountain of garbage

Spring: the old antique, she hasn't changed
    much for the better

—*Bai Ling*
[Translation by Eugene Eoyang on Taipei, Taiwan]

N.Y.

My City, my beloved, my white!
   Ah, slender,
Listen! Listen to me, and I will breath into thee
   a soul.
Delicately upon the reed, attend me!

Now do I know that I am mad,
For here are a million people surly with traffic;
This is no maid.
Neither could I play upon any reed if I had one.

My City, my beloved,
Thou art a maid with no breasts,
Thou art slender as a silver reed.
Listen to me, attend me!
And I will breathe into thee a soul,
And thou shalt live for ever.

—*Ezra Pound on New York City*

SHANGHAI '87

I follow a man and a thin woman up the stairs
of my mother's house. They are the first-floor
    family.
From a door on the second, a diminished woman
in a cotton gown watches. Hers is the room
my aunts slept in before they joined the trafiic
racing south, before the country shook its
    unbearable

holders. The house faces the road. Now an
    unbearable
clamor of bells and horns confuses the upstairs
muttering of women who no longer hear the traffic
hauling. Since the revolution, no family
member has reclaimed the house, twelve rooms
and a balcony. I'm a fresh intruder, a woman
who looks Chinese and claims to be child of a
    woman

named Chang. But my pronunciation is unbearable;
I was raised in the land of milk. Here is the room
my mother shared with brothers. We climb
    another stair
and I start to think in Chinese. All the family
to come will be born in English. Once, the traffic

of servants congested the landings; now the traffic
is of neighbors. From an oak-framed mirror,
    a woman
with my grandmother's face considers me.
    Her family
is about to disperse, the sons to travel unbearable
distances east. Her husband will descend the stairs
to a war. Now, in the master bedroom,
two children are directing toy trucks. The room
fills with Chinese sound effects and the traffic
of miniature pickups. From the upstairs

balcony, I can see a diving pool; a woman
or a man does laps. Through my first ten
  unbearable
Georgian summers, my mother took the family

swimming twice a week. She was ten when her
  family
left everything, the dogs, the domestics, the rooms
and banisters. In '66 a great aunt wrote of
  unbearable
climate. She did not mean heat. The clattering
  traffic
pauses and resumes. When I follow the thin woman
and her husband down the stairs,
the stairs complain. No one is left of the family.
All we have, the woman is saying, *is the first-floor
  room.*

Shanghai is crowded as Tokyo. The traffic is unbearable.

—Adrienne Su on Shanghai, China

THE DOUBLE CITY

I live in one city,
but then it becomes another.
The point where they mesh—
I call it mine.

Dacoits creep from caves
in the banks of the Indus.

One of them is displaced.
From Trafalgar Square
he dominates London, his face
masked by scarves and sunglasses.
He draws towards him all the conflict
of the metropolis—his speech
A barrage of grenades, rocket-launchers.

He marks time with his digital watch.
The pigeons get under his feet.

In the double city the beggar's cry
travels from one region to the next.

Under sapphire skies
or muscular clouds
there are fluid streets.
and solid streets
On some it is safe to walk.

The women of Southall
champion the release
of the battered Kiranjit
who killed her husband.
Lord Taylor, free her now!
Their saris billow in a storm of chants.
Schoolchildren of many nationalities
enact the Ramayana.

The Princely Rama
fights with demons
while the monkey god
searches for Princess Sita.

I make discoveries and lose them
little by little.
My journey in the double city
Starts beneath my feet.
You are here, says the arrow.

—*Moniza Alvi on London, England (and elsewhere)*

Readjustment of Twentieth-Century Space for Existence

Apartments and country places
Sit at the extremes of freeways
   And stare at each other
Going on in this deadlock
Is not as wise as slowing down
For the mountains have hilltops
   Houses have rooftops
And heaven would not give in to anyone
   Nor be lower than anyone
   No way
Those were the words of birds and planes
   On their way up there

In the days to come
As long as the freeways
   Are thoroughfares

There will be people bringing their idyll into town
And people driving their city into the country
Since soil and carpet have walked into
The same pair of shoes
And landscape and cityscape are equally pretty
In the same pair of eyes
Everybody will crowd into the TV set
   Not knowing each other
    But becoming faces all the more familiar

—*Luo Men (translation by Shiu-Pang Almberg)*

ABOUT THE POETS ❧

Adonis (1930–)

Ali Ahmed Said was born in Kassabin, Syria, in 1930. He adopted the name Adonis at the age of seventeen. He studied philosophy at Damascus University and at St. Joseph University in Beirut, earning Doctorat d'Etat in 1973. While exiled in Beirut in the 1960s, he co-founded the poetry magazine *Sh'ir*, and the review *Muwaqaf*. He has received the Syria-Lebanon Best Poet Award and the Brussels-based International Poem Biennial's highest award, among others. In addition to his poetic works, he has published numerous translations and essays, edited literary anthologies, and taught literature at many universities in the Middle East, Europe, and elsewhere. He lives in Paris at present.

Thomas Bailey Aldrich (1836–1907)

Thomas Bailey Aldrich was born in Portsmouth, New Hampshire, and grew up there, in New York, and in New Orleans. He went to work at the age of 16, after the death of his father, and by the time he was 19, he was working in New York as a professional writer and editor. He worked for several magazines there before leaving the city to become a war correspondent during the Civil War. In

1865, he moved to Boston, where he began to write poetry, short stories, and fiction. In the 1880s, Aldrich edited *The Atlantic Monthly*, and published more stories and volumes of poetry. At the time of his death, he was both a prolific and popular writer. Mark Twain attended his memorial service and mentioned Aldrich's "Story of a Bad Boy" as inspirational in writing *Huckleberry Finn*.

SHIU-PANG ALMBERG (TRANSLATOR)

Shiu-Pang Almberg is Associate Professor of Translation at the Chinese University of Hong Kong.

MONIZA ALVI (1954–)

Born in Lahore, Pakistan, Moniza Alvi moved to England when she was a few months old, with her Pakistani father and English mother. She grew up in Hertfordshire and studied at the universities of York and London. She now works as English Department Head at a secondary school in London. In 1991, she was the co-winner of the Poetry Business Prize. Her first full-length collection, *The Country at My Shoulder*, was selected for

The Poetry Society's "New Generation Poets" promotion. The poems in that collection referring to her Pakistani background are based on her childhood memories, family anecdotes, and flights of imagination. Later, she made her first return visit to Pakistan and went to India too; her impressions are at the heart of her second collection of poems, *A Bowl of Warm Air* (1996).

Antonio Manuel Bandeira (1886–1968)

Antonio Manuel Bandeira was born in Recife, Brazil, in 1886. He grew up in Recife and Rio de Janeiro, and planned to study architecture and engineering in São Paolo, but abandoned his studies due to poor health. He traveled to Greece and to Switzerland to recover from his severe tuberculosis, and stayed for over a year in a sanatorium in Clavadel, Switzerland. After his return to Brazil, he began publishing poetry and cultural criticism, establishing close ties with artists and writers active in the modernist movement in São Paolo. He has published many volumes of poetry, as well as works of literary history and cultural criticism. His poetry earned him a prize from the Brazilian Institute of Art and Culture in 1946, and he remained a prolific music, art, and literary critic up until his death in 1968.

BROTHER ANTHONY/AN SONJAE (TRANSLATOR)

Brother Anthony (An Sonjae) is Professor of Medieval and Renaissance Literature and Culture in the English Department of Sogang University, Seoul.

SUJATA BHATT (1956–)

Sujata Bhatt was born in Ahmedabad, India. She spent her childhood in Pune (Poona), India, as well as in New Orleans and in New Haven, Connecticut. She received her B.A. in Philosophy and English from Goucher College and her M.F.A. from the Writers' Workshop at the University of Iowa. She has published six collections of poetry (including a *Selected Poems*) with Carcanet Press, U.K. Several of her books have also been published by Penguin, India. She has received numerous awards for her work, such as the Alice Hunt Bartlett Award, the Commonwealth Poetry Prize, the Cholmondeley Award, and, most recently, the Italian Tratti Poetry Prize. Her work has been widely anthologized, translated into more than a dozen languages, and is regularly broadcast on BBC radio and television. She works as a full-time writer (in Bremen, Germany, where she usually lives) and is a frequent guest at international literary festivals throughout the world.

WILLIAM BLAKE (1757–1827)

William Blake was born in London in 1757, where he learned to read and write at home. Apart from briefly studying in an arts school, Blake receive little formal education. He started studying drawing at age ten, and began writing poetry by the age of twelve. He began a seven-year apprenticeship with an engraver at the age of fourteen. During this time, he continued work on his *Poetical Sketches* (1783), a collection of poems that mixed mysticism with social critique. His best-known collection of poems, *Songs of Innocence*, was published in 1789, followed by *The Marriage of Heaven and Hell* in 1790–1793, and *Songs of Experience* in 1794. At the time of his death in 1827, Blake was working on a series of illustrations of Dante's *Divine Comedy* for which he had received a commission.

KAMAU BRATHWAITE (1930–)

Kamau Brathwaite was born in Bridgetown, Barbados, on May 11, 1930. He was educated at Harrison College (Barbados) before earning a B.A. with honors in 1953 and a Diploma of Education in 1954, both from Pembroke College, Cambridge. He left England for Africa to pursue a career in education, and worked for several years in Ghana. He received a Doctorate in Philosophy from the University of Sussex (1968), and subsequently divided his time between writing and teaching, mainly at the University of the West Indies in Mona, Jamaica. His writings span a wide range of topics, from sociolinguistics to Caribbean cultural history, and embrace both nonfiction and poetry. Among his works in poetry are the *The Arrivants: A New World Trilogy* (1973), the collections *Black and Blues* (1976) and *Trenchtown Rock* (1993), and his most recent publication *Words Need Love Too* (2002).

WILLIAM CULLEN BRYANT (1794–1878)

William Cullen Bryant was born in Massachusetts, where he worked as a lawyer, poet, critic, and editor. He went to work for the *New York Evening Post* in 1825, and later became its editor. He is celebrated for such works as *Thanatopsis*, *To a Waterfowl*, and *The Embargo* (1808). He translated both *The Iliad* and *The Odyssey* in the 1870s.

BLAISE CENDRARS (1887–1961)

Blaise Cendrars was born Frèdèric Sauser in Switzerland. His choice of pseudonym suggests, according to L. C. Breunig, "poetry as a process of combustion." Cendrars was a world traveler, spending years traversing Europe, Asia, and the Americas. Much of his poetry and prose chronicles his stays in California, New York, Panama, and French Guyana, among other places. Years later, he returned to Europe, living in the south of France (during World War II) and then in Paris for the rest of his life.

ALICE CORBIN (1881–1949)

Alice Corbin was born in St. Louis and attended the University of Chicago. She was an associate editor of *Poetry: A Magazine of Verse* since its founding in 1912. She also co-edited an anthology of modern English and American poets titled *The New Poetry*. Corbin is the author of the verse plays *Adam's Dream and Two Other Miracle Plays for Children*, and of a collection of poems, *The Spinning Woman of the Sky*.

JONATHAN CHAVES (TRANSLATOR)

Jonathan Chaves is Chair of the Department of East Asian Languages and Literatures and Professor of Chinese at George Washington University.

ANN Y. CHOI

Ann Choi's poems have been published in *Ploughshares*, *jubilat*, and *Amerasia Journal*, among others. Her first book of poetry, *New Country*, is forthcoming. She was educated at Smith College and UCLA, and now teaches at Rutgers University.

John Davidson (1857–1909)

John Davidson was born in Scotland in 1857, where he lived and taught for most of his life. He moved to London in 1889 and began working as a journalist, publishing articles, poems, novels, and translations. His book of poetry, *Fleet Street Eclogues* (1893), earned T. S. Eliot's admiration. Eliot later wrote a preface to Davidson's posthumously published *Selected Poems* (1961). He moved from London to Penzance in 1907. After struggling financially in both London and Penzance, and battling illness and depression in his last years, Davidson committed suicide in 1909.

Enid Derham (1882–1941)

Enid Derham was born and educated in Melbourne, Australia. She taught English at Melbourne University between 1922 and 1941. In 1912 she published *The Mountain Road and Other Verses* and *Empire* (a children's play).

Mark Doty (1953–)

Mark Doty is the author of six books of poems, and has earned numerous literary prizes and fellowships for his writing. His third book of poetry, *My Alexandria* (1993), was chosen by Philip Levine for the National Poetry Series, and also won the

National Book Critics Circle Award and Britain's T. S. Eliot Prize. He has also published *Heaven's Coast: A Memoir* (1996), which won the PEN/ Martha Allbrand Award for First Nonfiction. He has received fellowships from the Guggenheim, Ingram Merrill, Rockefeller, and Whiting foundations, and from the National Endowment for the Arts. He lives in Provincetown, Massachusetts, and in Houston, Texas, where he teaches in the University of Houston graduate creative writing program.

Eugene Eoyang (Translator)

Professor of English at Lingnan College, Hong Kong, Eugene Eoyang has lectured and taught at Indiana University and at University of Illinois, Champaign-Urbana.

Chester Firkins (1882–1915)

Chester Firkins was born in Minneapolis, Minnesota. He worked as a journalist in Columbus and Cincinnati, Ohio, and in Chicago, Illinois, before moving to New York City, where he joined the staff of the *New York American*. He worked there until his death on March 1, 1915. Many of his stories and poems were published in magazines, and a volume of his poems was published posthumously in 1916.

Thomas Hardy (1840–1928)

Thomas Hardy was born in Dorset, England, in 1840. He trained as an architect, working in London and Dorset for ten years. He began writing novels, publishing *Desperate Remedies* in 1871, and soon gave up architecture for full-time writing. After publishing the novels *Tess of the D'Urbervilles* and *Jude the Obscure*, Hardy produced eight collections of poetry, including *Wessex Poems* (1898) and *Satires of Circumstance* (1912).

Thomas Hood (1799–1845)

Born in London to a Scottish bookseller father, Thomas Hood was raised there until he was sent to Dundee in 1815 because of his poor health. He returned to London in 1818, and worked as an engraver until he became a sub-editor of *London Magazine* in 1821. While working there, Hood met such writers as Hazlitt and Lamb. In 1829, Hood went on to become editor of another magazine, *The Gem*, in which he published writings by Tennyson. Better known in his lifetime for his comic writings, Hood's serious work has since earned him more attention. His poem, "The Song of the Shirt," a critique of workers' exploitation, was published anonymously in *Punch* in 1843. It was made into a play called *The Sempstress*, and was printed on broadsheets and cotton handkerchiefs. It was praised by many of his contemporary writers, including Charles Dickens. Hood depicts his childhood in the poem "I Remember, I Remember," which is said to have inspired the poet Philip Larkin to write a poem of the same title.

Gerard Manley Hopkins (1844–1889)

Born in Stratford, England, in 1844, Gerard Manley Hopkins is regarded as one of the Victorian era's greatest poets. He studied classics at Balliol College, Oxford. In 1866, Hopkins converted to Catholicism and in 1867, he entered a Jesuit novitiate near London to study for the priesthood. Hopkins burned all of the poetry he had previously written and would not write poems again until 1875. In his first poem written after this period, titled "The Wreck of the Deutschland," Hopkins introduced what he called "sprung rhythm," a metrical form that would be famously linked to his name. In 1884, Hopkins moved to Dublin to take a teaching position, and he died there five years later. His poems were published posthumously in a collection released in 1918.

Shahid Hosain (1934–)

Born in Aligarh, Khwaja, Shahid Hosain was among the earliest Pakistani poets to write in English. He edited the first anthology of Pakistani poetry in English, *First Voices: Six Poets from Pakistan* (1965), in which his own work also appeared. His later poetry was published in *Pieces of Eight* (1971), and *Pakistani Literature: The Contemporary English Writers* (1978). As a civil servant, he was closely associated with the development of films and the electronic media in Pakistan. He moved to London and set up Hosain's, an antiquarian bookshop. At present, he is Pakistan's ambassador to UNESCO.

VICENTE HUIDOBRO (1893–1948)

Vicente Huidobro was born in Santiago, Chile, in 1893. At the age of twenty-three, Huidobro moved to Paris and became involved with the Cubist movement, co-editing a review titled *Nord-Sud* with the poet Pierre Reverdy. Many of Huidobro's poems were included in this review, and the two editors' styles were so closely linked that translator L. C. Breunig remarks, "it is at times difficult to distinguish between the two." Huidobro continued to publish his work in Paris until 1925, when he released his last work in French, *Tout à Coup (All of a Sudden)*. He returned to Chile that year, where he went on to write poetry in Spanish. By the time of his death in 1948, Huidobro has gained recognition as "one of the major Latin American poets of the twentieth century."

RASHID HUSAIN (1936–1977)

A poet from a Muslim village near Haifa, Husain first worked as a schoolteacher, but was dismissed by the Israelis for his political beliefs. An organizer of the Al-Ard party in Israel, which was founded in 1958 and later banned, he spent many years in Israeli prisons. He became an editor of the Arab journal *Al-Fajr (The Dawn)*, which was banned in 1962. He translated selections from Hayyim Bialik's poetry from Hebrew into Arabic and translated Palestinian folk songs into Hebrew. After the June 1967 war, he went into exile and lived in poverty in New York City, dying in a fire in his apartment. Husain's poetry is mainly concerned with the predicament of Palestinians under siege both in Israel and in the diaspora. He has published three collections of poetry, the last of which is *I Am the Land, Don't Deprive Me of the Rain*.

ROBIN HYDE (1906–1939)

Robin Hyde was born in Cape Town and brought to Wellington, New Zealand, as a baby. She briefly studied at Victoria University College, and then worked as a journalist for a number of local and national newspapers. Her first book of poetry, *The Desolate Star and Other Poems*, was published in 1929. In her autobiographical novel, *The Godwits* (1938), she wrote about poverty and marginalization from her personal and familial experience of it, as well as from her journalistic experiences. On January 18, 1938, Hyde sailed on the *SS Changte*, intending to go to England. Arriving in Hong Kong, she made the momentous decision to travel to China, which was then at war with Japan. She traveled to the war front, the first female journalist to do so, and despite a perilous assault by Japanese soldiers she succeeded in reaching Tsingtao and then Hong Kong. On August 23, 1939, Hyde killed herself by taking poison.

Rashidah Ismaili (1941–)

Rashidah Ismaili was born in Cotonou, Benin. She was first educated in a Quranic school run by her maternal grandmother. After leaving Africa for Italy and France to avoid an arranged marriage, she went to New York, where she studied music and then earned an M.A. in social psychology and a Ph.D. in psychology from the New School. She has published several volumes of poetry, among them *Oniybo and Other Poems* and *Missing in Action and Presumed Dead*.

May Jayyusi (Translator)

May Jayyusi has published numerous translations of Arabic-language fiction and poetry.

Rudyard Kipling (1865–1936)

Joseph Rudyard Kipling was born in Bombay, India, in 1865, to a British family. At the age of five, he was sent to England for his education. He returned to India at seventeen and began working as a journalist and editor for the *Civil and Military Gazette* in Lahore (now Pakistan). In 1886, he published his first collection of poems, *Departmental Ditties and Other Verses*, and in 1888 published his first collection of stories, *Plain Tales from the Hills*. He published another book of poems, *Barrack-Room Ballads* in 1892, which contained the highly popular poems "Gunga Din" and "Mandalay." In 1892, Kipling married and moved to Vermont, where he published the two *Jungle Book*s and began work on *Kim*. He returned to England with his family in 1896 and published the novel *Captains Courageous*. During the Boer War, Kipling visited South Africa, editing a newspaper there for a while and writing his *Just-So Stories*. *Kim*, Kipling's last novel, appeared in 1901. In 1902, Kipling and his family moved to Sussex, where he spent the rest of his life writing poetry and short stories, including one of his most famous poems, "If."

Henry Lawson (1867–1922)

Henry Lawson was born near Grenfell, New South Wales, on June 17, 1867. His father was Norwegian and his mother's family was from New South Wales. He worked with his father as a farmer and contractor before moving to Sydney and training as a coach-painter. He began writing poetry in the late 1880s, subsequently joining the staff of the Queensland *Boomerang* in 1890. He traveled throughout Australia and New Zealand, and as far as London in 1900, returning to Sydney in 1903, where he lived the rest of his years.

Nicholas Vachel Lindsay (1879–1931)

Nicholas Vachel Lindsay, or Vachel Lindsay as he was better known, was born in Springfield, Illinois, in 1879. He attended Hiram College in Ohio before moving to Chicago and New York to study art. After writing poetry for a short time, he earned initial recognition with *Poetry* magazine's 1913 publication of his poem "General William Booth Enters into Heaven," about the founder of the Salvation Army. Lindsay's later poem, "The Congo," became one of his best-known works. He spent much of his life walking across the country, performing and distributing copies of his poetry in exhange for room and board. Lindsay settled into his family home in Springfield in 1929, and became severely depressed shortly thereafter. In 1931, he committed suicide by drinking poison.

BAI LING (1951–)

Bai Ling (Pai Ling, or "White Spirit") is the pen name of Zhuang Zhuang, who was born in Taipei, Taiwan. He graduated from the Taipei Institute of Technology and received an M.S. in chemical engineering from Stevens College of Science and Engineering in New Jersey. Currently he is an associate professor at the Taipei Institute of Technology. Bai Ling joined the Grape Orchard Poetry Society in the 1960s, and later the Grass Roots Poetry Society in the 1970s. In 1985, he co-founded the city's Sound and Light Workshop with fellow poets Luo Qing and Du Shisan, and experimented with multimedia performances of poetry. He is also a co-founder of the *Taiwan Poetics Quarterly*. To date, he has published four books of poetry in addition to prose and literary criticism.

HENRY WADSWORTH LONGFELLOW (1807–1882)

Henry Wadsworth Longfellow was born in Portland, Maine (then still part of Massachusetts) on February 27, 1807. In the early 1830s, he published his first book, a travelogue called *Outre Mer (Overseas)*, and began teaching at Harvard in 1836. Three years later, Longfellow published his first collection of poems, *Voices of the Night*, followed in 1841 by *Ballads and Other Poems*. In 1854, Longfellow quit teaching to devote all his time to writing poetry. He published *Hiawatha* and *The Courtship of Miles Standish* during this time. Just before the start of the Civil War, Longfellow wrote "Paul Revere's Ride," and *Tales of a Wayside Inn* (said to have been written before his wife's death in 1861, but published in 1863). From 1866 on, Longfellow produced seven more books of poetry. His seventy-fifth birthday was celebrated across the country in 1882, and he died shortly after.

Robert Lowell (1917–1977)

Robert Lowell was born in Boston in 1917, and attended Harvard University and Kenyon College, graduating from the latter in 1940. In his under-graduate and graduate years, he studied with John Crowe Ransom, Robert Penn Warren, and Cleanth Brooks. Lowell was the author of many books of poems, plays, and translations. He was a public voice against both World War II and the Vietnam War, as a conscientious objector during the former and a vocal opponent of the latter. Lowell suffered for much of his life from manic depression, for which he was hospitalized repeatedly. He died at the age of sixty in New York City.

Louis MacNeice (1907–1963)

Louis MacNeice was born in Belfast, Ireland (now Northern Ireland), in 1907. He was educated in

England at Marlborough and at Oxford, where he received a B.A. degree. Before the start of World War II, he taught classics at the universities of Birmingham and London, and at Cornell University. Returning to England in 1940, he became a producer for the BBC. In addition to his radio plays, translations, critical work, and autobiographical writings, MacNeice published sixteen books of poetry. His *Collected Poems* (1966) appeared three years after his death in London.

Louise Mack (1870–1935)

Louise Mack was born in Hobart, Tasmania, to Irish parents. Her first novel, *The World is Round*, was published in London in 1896. The following year, her book, *Teens: A Story of Australian Schoolgirls*, was published in Sydney. Moving to London in 1901, Mack published several more books there, including *An Australian Girl in London*. After relocating to Florence, Italy, she worked as editor of the *Italian Gazette*, and went on to become the first female war correspondent for the London newspapers *The Daily Mail* and *The Evening News*.

Luo Men (1928–)

The poet and critic Luo Men has lived in and written about Taiwan and its cities for nearly fifty years. He is described by critic Kuo-ch'ing Tu as

"obsessed with the exploration of 'urban literature.' "
Since his publication of *Dushi de Ren (People in the City)* in 1957, he has been "writing 'dushi shi' (urban poetry), [and] exploring themes having to do with the city...."

EDWIN MORGAN (1920–)

Edwin George Morgan was born in Glasgow, Scotland, in 1920. He grew up in Rutherglen and went on to high school and university in Glasgow, interrupting his studies at Glasgow University to join the Royal Army Medical Corps. He returned to university in 1946, graduating the following year and remaining in Glasgow to teach. His work embraces a wide variety of forms and themes, from sonnets to concrete poetry to collaborations with musicians and composers. He has translated numerous works of literature from French, Russian, Hungarian, Spanish, and other languages, among them a highly acclaimed version of Rostand's *Cyrano de Bergerac* and Racine's *Phèdre* (which won the Weidenfeld Prize for Translation), both published by Carcanet. He was Glasgow's Poet Laureate for 1999.

LES MURRAY (1938–)

Leslie Allan Murray was born October 17, 1938, in Bunyah, New South Wales. He attended the

University of Sydney and served in the Royal Australian Naval Reserve. His most recent book, *Freddy Neptune: A Novel in Verse*, treats the picaresque life of German-Australian sailor Freidrich Boettcher, "a kind of Nordic hero who witnesses and records, in demotic style, the foibles of his age." His previous collection, *Subhuman Redneck Poem*, was awarded the 1996 T. S. Eliot Prize. Murray lives in his native Bunyah.

NAOMI SHIHAB NYE (TRANSLATOR)

Naomi Shihab Nye was born to a Palestinian father and an American mother, and grew up in St. Louis, Jerusalem, and San Antonio. Among the many books she has written and/or edited are: *19 Varieties of Gazelle: Poems of the Middle East, Fuel (Poems), Never in a Hurry* (a collection of essays), *Habibi* (a novel for young readers), and *Lullaby Raft* (a picture book). She has been a Lannan Fellow, a Guggenheim Fellow, and a Wittner Bynner Fellow (Library of Congress). She has received an award from the Academy of American Poets, four Pushcart Prizes, and numerous other honors. She has been featured on two PBS poetry specials: "The Language of Life, with Bill Moyers" and "The United States of Poetry."

Octavio Paz (1914–1998)

Octavio Paz was born in Mexico City in 1914. By the time he was nineteen, Paz had founded a literary journal and published his first book of poems, titled *Savage Moon* (1933). His poetry is known for its treatment of ancient and contemporary Mexican civilization and for its incorporation of many formal and thematic elements of the Surrealist and Modernist movements. He founded several influential journals, among them an international literary magazine called *Vuelta (Return)*, which thrived well into the 1980s. His study of modern Mexican society, *The Labyrinth of Solitude*, was published to great acclaim in 1950, and was followed by several well-received volumes of poetry. In 1962, he was named Mexico's ambassador to India, where he was posted for six years. In 1968, after the Mexican government suppressed a university demonstration and killed many students, Paz resigned his post in protest. In 1982, he won Spain's highest literary honor, the Cervantes, and in 1990 he was awarded the Nobel Prize for Literature.

Ezra Pound (1885–1972)

Ezra Pound was born in Hailey, Idaho, in 1885. He attended the University of Pennsylvania for two years and earned his B.A. from Hamilton College in 1905. After teaching at Wabash College for two years, Pound traveled to Spain, Italy, and London, where he became interested in Chinese and Japanese poetry. In 1924, he settled in Italy. During this period of self-imposed exile, he became involved in Fascist politics, remaining in Europe throughout World War II. He was charged with treason on his return to the United States, for having broadcast Fascist propaganda during the war. He was acquitted in 1946, but was declared mentally ill and committed to St. Elizabeth's Hospital in Washington, D.C. After his release from the hospital in 1958, Pound returned to Italy and settled in Venice, where he remained until his death in 1972.

CARL SANDBURG (1878–1967)

Carl Sandburg was born in Galesburg, Illinois, in 1878. He spent most of his life traveling and living in the Midwest, where he worked as a delivery person, a bricklayer, a wheat-thresher, and a shoe-shiner, eventually spending the year 1897 traveling as a hobo. These experiences found their way into his writing, which encompassed everything from folk songs to journalistic articles to poetry. He went on to settle in Chicago and wrote on labor issues for the *Chicago Daily News*. In 1919, he published a book of his articles, *The Chicago Race Riots*, and went on to write more poems, short stories, and articles. He published one novel, *Remembrance*

Rock, when he was seventy, as well as numerous volumes of biography. His four-volume biography of Abraham Lincoln, *Abraham Lincoln: The War Years*, earned him the Pulitzer Prize in History. In 1945, Sandburg moved with his family to Flat Rock, North Carolina, where he remained until his death in 1967.

Duncan Campbell Scott (1862–1947)

Duncan Campbell Scott wrote mainly about the relationship between man and nature, and about Native American life in his home country of Canada. He worked for the Canadian government for most of his adult life.

Suh Sook (Translator)

Suh Sook is a professor in the English Department of Ewha Womans University in Seoul, Korea.

Wole Soyinka (1934–)

Born Akinwande Oluwole Soyinka in Abeukuta, Nigeria, Wole Soyinka is perhaps best known as an internationally acclaimed playwright. He has also published many collections of essays and poetry, as well as novels. His early life is recounted in *Ake: The Years of Childhood* (1981), and in *Isara: A Voyage*

Around "Essay" (1989). He founded a theater company, 1960 Masks, which produced *A Dance of the Forests,* his first major play. In October 1965, Soyinka was arrested for allegedly seizing the Western Region radio studios and making a political broadcast disputing the recently published election results. He then served as director of the Drama School of Ibadan University in Nigeria until 1967, when he was arrested for writings sympathetic to secessionist Biafra. He was imprisoned for twenty-two months, and wrote about his experiences in *Madmen and Specialists* (1970) shortly after his release. In 1978, Soyinka founded another theater company, called the Unife Guerilla Theatre, which presented plays and sketches in markets, in parks, and on street corners. The plays attacked the endemic corruption and political oppression of contemporary Nigeria, critiques that were paralleled in Soyinka's articles and essays. Soyinka's writings about the regime of dictator Sani Abacha, who seized power in 1993 from the presumed election winner Mashood Abiola, forced him into exile from 1994 until Abacha's death in 1998. Soyinka continued to protest the human rights abuses of the regime throughout this period. He currently divides his time between writing and teaching in Nigeria and in universities overseas.

Robert Louis Stevenson (1850–1894)

Born in Edinburgh, Robert Louis Stevenson studied engineering and then law at the University of Edinburgh. From his youth, Stevenson suffered from tuberculosis and often traveled to warmer climates for his health. Some of his journeys are depicted in his early works, such as *An Inland Voyage* (1878) and *Travels With a Donkey in the Cévennes* (1879), which recounted his travels through Belgium and France. In 1879, he traveled to California, where he married an American in 1880. The couple settled in Samoa in 1889, where Stevenson died five years later. His best known works are his adventure novels *Treasure Island* (1883), *Kidnapped* (1886), and the horror story *The Strange Case of Dr. Jekyll and Mr. Hyde* (1886).

Adrienne Su

Adrienne Su is Assistant Professor of English at Dickinson College, where she has taught poetry writing, contemporary poetry, Asian-American literature, "Writing about Food and Culture," and a freshman seminar on Carlisle, Pennsylvania's Old Pomfret Street Farmers' Market. She studied at Harvard and the University of Virginia, and is the author of the poetry book *Middle Kingdom*.

JONATHAN SWIFT (1667–1745)

Jonathan Swift was born to English parents in Dublin, where he grew up and graduated from Kilkenny School and Trinity College. Swift's satires did not spare the church, but his most famous works, such as *Gulliver's Travels*, *A Modest Proposal*, and *The Drapier's Letters* were more broadly directed at Irish and English society and government (and their religious institutions). In 1713, he became Dean of St. Patrick's Cathedral in Dublin, and held that post until the effects of his Meuniere's disease prevented him from fulfilling his duties. He died in Dublin in 1745, and is buried in St. Patrick's.

JOHN ADDINGTON SYMONDS (1840–1893)

Educated at Harrow and at Oxford, John Addington Symonds's many writings include the travel books *Sketches in Italy and Greece* (1874) and *Italian Byways* (1883), literary essays such as *Introduction to the Study of Dante* (1872) and *Studies of Greek Poets* (1873–1876), biographies of Michelangelo, Jonson, Shelley, and Sidney, and many volumes of verse. Among these are his *Many Moods* (1878) and *Animi Figura* (1882). He also produced a seven-volume work of cultural history titled *The Renaissance in Italy* (1875–1886).

ABDULLAH AL-UDHARI (TRANSLATOR)

Abdullah al-Udhari was born in Taiz, Yemen, and has worked for over thirty years as a poet, translator, and literary historian.

DEREK WALCOTT (1930–)

Derek Walcott was born in Saint Lucia in 1930, and began writing poetry at the age of eighteen. He graduated from the University of the West Indies, and in 1957 was awarded a Rockefeller Foundation fellowship to study American theater. He is the founder of the Trinidad Theater Workshop, and has written and directed many plays. His 1971 play, *Dream on Monkey Mountain*, won the Obie Award for distinguished foreign play of that year, and he has received a MacArthur Foundation "Genius" award (in 1981), a Royal Society of Literature Award, and the Queen's Medal for Poetry (in 1988). He received the Nobel Prize for Literature in 1992. Walcott teaches poetry and playwriting at Boston University every fall and lives the rest of the year in Saint Lucia.

EUGENE FITCH WARE, "IRONQUILL" (1841–1911)

Eugene Fitch Ware was born in Hartford, Connecticut, in 1841. His parents moved to Burlington,

Iowa, when he was a child, and he was educated in the public schools there. In 1861, he enlisted in the army, serving as an infantryman, cavalryman, and aide-de-camp to various generals until 1866. In 1867, he took a section of land in Cherokee territory in Kansas, studied law, and was admitted to the bar and served for many years as the editor of the *Fort Scott Monitor*. He was elected to the state legislature twice, and served for three years as the U.S. pension commissioner (1902–1905). He was a delegate to two of the Republican National Conventions, and practiced law in Fort Scott, Kansas.

Walt Whitman (1819–1892)

Born May 31, 1819, Walt Whitman grew up in Brooklyn and Long Island, New York, in the 1820s and 1830s. He worked as a printer in New York City until 1836, when, at the age of seventeen, he began teaching in Long Island. He taught until 1841, when he turned to journalism, leaving New York in 1848 to edit *The Crescent*, a daily newspaper in New Orleans. It was in New Orleans that Whitman saw the slave markets, and where he began work on *Leaves of Grass*. He published the first edition of *Leaves of Grass* in 1855, when it comprised twelve untitled poems and a preface.

After his death on March 26, 1892, Whitman was buried in a tomb that he had designed and built in Harleigh Cemetery in Camden, New Jersey.

Oscar Wilde (1854–1900)

Born on October 16, 1854, in Dublin, Oscar Fingal O'Flahertie Wills Wilde spent his childhood and college years in Dublin. After attending Trinity College from 1870 to 1874, he studied at Magdalen College, Oxford. Wilde's fame grew with the publication of *The Picture of Dorian Gray* and of several of his essays (including "The Decay of Lying") in 1891. That year, he also met Lord Alfred Douglas, whose father, the Marquess of Queensbury, strongly objected to his son's relationship with Wilde. In 1895, Queensbury charged Wilde with sodomy, and Wilde sued him for criminal libel. After Queensbury was acquitted, Wilde was charged under the 1885 Criminal Law Amendment Act, and was subjected to two new trials. At the second trial, Wilde was sentenced to two years' imprisonment and hard labor. While in prison, Wilde wrote *De Profundis*, which was not published until after his death. After his release, Wilde moved to France, where he was briefly reunited with Douglas. Wilde died of cerebral meningitis in Paris in 1900.

WILLIAM WORDSWORTH (1770–1850)

William Wordsworth was born on April 7, 1770, in the village of Cockermouth, Cumbria, England. Wordsworth's mother died when he was eight, a loss that is said to have shaped much of his later work. He attended Hawkshead Grammar School, where it is believed that he developed his love of poetry, and began to compose his own. Wordsworth was orphaned while still in grammar school, along with his four siblings. He managed to continue his schooling, going on to study at St. John's College, Cambridge. He left before his final semester to embark on a walking tour of Europe, and his experiences on this journey find their expression in his poetry. His earliest poetry was published in 1793 in the collections *An Evening Walk* and *Descriptive Sketches.* In 1798, Wordsworth and his close friend Samuel Taylor Coleridge published jointly (and anonymously) their *Lyrical Ballads. The Prelude* (1850), perhaps his best known work, was not published until after he died.

CH'ON YANG-HUI (1942–)

Born in Pusan, Korea, in 1942, Ch'on Yang-hui began her career as a poet in 1962. In that year, her poetry appeared in the review *Hyondae Munhak (Modern Literature).* She graduated from Ewha Womans University in 1966 and did not publish a complete volume of poems until 1983, when she produced *Shini Uridurege Mudnundamion* (*If God Asks Us*). Her most recent volume of poems, *Yetkolmokkil (An Old Alley)*, appeared in 1998. Her work received the tenth Seoul Poetry Award, and she also received the forty-third *Hyondae Munhok* (Modern Literature) Prize.

PERMISSIONS ACKNOWLEDGMENTS ❧

AUTHOR INDEX ❧

Addington, John 182
Adonis 89
Aldrich, Thomas Bailey 3
Alvi, Moniza 236
Bandeira, Antonio Manuel 148
Bhatt, Sujata 74
Blake, William 83
Brathwaite, Kamau 16
Bryant, William Cullen 137
Cendrars, Blaise 13
Choi, Ann 132
Coll, Aloysius 216
Corbin, Alice 6
Davidson, John 47
Derham, Enid 155
Doty, Mark 114
Firkins, Chester 10
Hardy, Thomas 194
Hood, Thomas 140
Hopkins, Gerard Manley 195
Hosain, Shahid 87
Huidobro, Vicente 222
Husain, Rashid 80
Hyde, Robin 45
Ismaili, Rashidah 68
Jones, Ruth Lambert 136

Kipling, Rudyard 84, 197
Lawson, Henry 123
Lindsay, Vichel 212
Ling, Bai 227
Longfellow, Henry Wadsworth 187
Lowell, Robert 205
Mack, Louise 180
MacNeice, Louis 201
Men, Luo 239
Morgan, Edwin 32
Murray, Les 118
Paz, Octavio 159
Piao-yüan, Tai 122
Pound, Ezra 231
Sandburg, Carl 42
Scott, Duncan Campbell 157
Soyinka, Wole 48
Stevenson, Robert Louis 2
Su, Adrienne 232
Swift, Jonathan 28, 218
Walcott, Derek 146
Ware, Eugene Fitch ("Ironquill") 184
Whitman, Walt 209
Wilde, Oscar 26
Wordsworth, William 158
Yang-Hui, Ch'on 24

CITY INDEX ॐ

Ahmedabad, India 74
Bamako, Mali 16
Beirut, Lebanon 89
Buenos Aires, Argentina 205
Chicago, Illinois 42
Damascus, Syria 80
Dublin, Ireland 201
Glasgow, Scotland 32
Hong Kong, China 45
Kabul, Afghanistan 84
Lagos, Nigeria 68
Lahore, Pakistan 87
London, England 26, 28, 47, 83, 158, 236
Melbourne, Australia 155
Mexico City, Mexico 159
New York, New York 114, 209, 231
Nuremberg, Germany 187

Ottawa, Canada 157
Oxford, England 195
Paris, France 13, 222
Philadelphia, Pennsylvania 197
Port-of-Spain, Trinidad 146
Recife, Brazil 148
Rome, Italy 194
Rotterdam, The Netherlands 140
Samarkand, Uzbekistan 48
Seoul, Korea 24, 132
Shanghai, China 232
Spain, cities 3
Springfield, Illinois 212
Sydney, Australia 118, 180
T'ung-ch'uan, China 122
Taipei, Taiwan 230
Venice, Italy 182
Washington, D.C. 216